MW00979783

By the same author

• Seeing the Light of World Faith

• Light After Death

• Enlightened Views

FANATICISM
A World-Devouring Fire

Alan Bryson

STERLING PUBLISHERS PRIVATE LIMITED

STERLING PUBLISHERS PRIVATE LIMITED
A-59 Okhla Industrial Area, Phase-II,
New Delhi-110020.
Tel: 6916209, 6916165, 6912677, 6910050
Fax: 91-11-6331241 E-mail: ghai@nde.vsnl.net.in
www.sterlingpublishers.com

Fanaticism: A World-Devouring Fire
© 2002, *Alan Bryson*
ISBN 81 207 2463 1

All rights are reserved. No part of this publication may be reproduced, stored in a retrieval system or transmitted, in any form or by any means, mechanical, photocopying, recording or otherwise, without prior written permission of the original publisher.

PRINTED IN INDIA

Published by Sterling Publishers Pvt. Ltd., New Delhi-110 020.
Lasertypeset at Vikas Compographics, New Delhi-110020.
Printed at Prolific Incorporated, New Delhi-110020.

Foreword

The work produced by Mr. Alan Bryson, a member of the Bahá'í Faith in Germany, could not have been more timely. Last year's Black Tuesday in September and Miraculous Thursday in December and this year's carnage and communal violence in Gujarat are indicative of the signs and portents of present-day society. The phenomenon is worldwide. There is steady and general deterioration in the quality of life everywhere not simply due to the economic disparities and injustices, not even due to the worsening conditions of the environment but primarily due to suspicion, fear, and hatred throughout the world. How apt, therefore, is this passage from the Bahá'í writings penned over a century ago. "Today we have closed our eyes to every righteous act and have sacrificed the abiding happiness of society to our own transitory profit. We regard fanaticism and zealotry as redounding to our credit and honour, and not content with this, we denounce one another and plot each other's ruin, and whenever we wish to put on a show of wisdom and learning, of virtue and godliness, we set about mocking and reviling this one and that."

Indeed, as the Universal House of Justice noted in November of 1992, "the world in its current condition has lost its bearings through the operation of forces it neither understands nor can control. It is a period in which great dynasties and empires have collapsed in rapid succession, in which powerful ideologies have captured the hearts of millions only to expire in infamy, in which two world wars wreaked havoc on civilised life as it was known at the beginning of the 20th century." The trend shows no signs of abating. International terrorism, insurgency and militancy, internal and external threats and countless other destructive activities have filled with fear and dismay the hearts and minds of all thoughtful citizens in every country. Coping with day-to-day chores with such rampant uncertainty has deranged the world's equilibrium. Added to this are the genocides and well conceived pogroms of ethnic and minority community cleansing. The tumult and upheaval is universal. One day it is Fiji, the next day could be Kosovo, Somalia. Or it could be Chechnya or Afghanistan. The list is unending. The questions that beget us are: Who is responsible? Whither are we headed? The Taliban has been temporarily wiped out, the Al Qaeda have been scattered, but Islamic *jehadis* continue to operate in large numbers. O how shameful it has become for an ordinary Muslim to face his fellow non-Muslims in any society.

The book provides a context, a rich tapestry of scriptural quotes pertinent to the overall theme of fanaticism and offers plausible answers for coming out of present-day deadlocks. It calls for a searching re-examination of the prevailing patterns of societal organisation be it social, economic, religious or political. The author suggests that it is no longer possible to maintain the belief that the well-being of the planet's inhabitants and progress of the nations can occur simply on basis of the materialistic conception of life.

Most importantly the appeal is to the religious leadership, especially the Muslim religious leaders to educate and prevail upon the masses of their followers to turn away from prejudice and fanaticism so that present-day civilisation may be saved from the slough of impending extinction. My heart aches, for I note with intense regret that the attention of the people at the helm of affairs is nowhere directed toward that which is worthy of this day and time. Please God let a new beginning be made.

New Delhi   **Dr. A. K. Merchant**
May 09, 2002

Contents

Surely if living creatures saw the results of all their
evil deeds,
they would turn away from them in disgust.
Buddha

... him that loveth violence his soul hateth.
Book of Psalms

Do those who commit evil deeds count
that we will make them like those who believe
and work righteous deeds,
equal in their life and their death?
- ill it is they judge.
Qu'rán

A man should not hate any living creature.
Let him be friendly and compassionate to all.
Krishna, Bhagavad-Gita

This is my commandment, that ye love one another...
Jesus

The sinner and deluded man may succeed at first
and even attain high renown for his evil deeds,
but Ye, O Lord of Life, are well aware of everything
and shall judge the deeds of everyone
from his or her motives through Thy Wisdom.
Zoroaster

Introduction

On September 11, 2001, billions of people around the globe watched in shock and dismay as horrific scenes of mass murder unfolded before their eyes. In an instant, men with hearts as hard as stone and souls as black as night, callously murdered thousands of innocent men, women and children. In the ninth month of the first year of a new millennium, mankind's hopes for a new and peaceful future appeared to crumble into a smouldering mass grave only blocks away from the headquarters of the United Nations. After it was discovered that the attack was perpetrated by fanatics claiming to act in the name of God, this appallingly reprehensible act became even more abhorrent. The extent of their fanaticism gave chilling notice that conciliation, appeasement, and reason would only fan the flames of their fury. Among their final instructions, were calls to bathe carefully, remove excess body hair, and repeat a thousand times, "There is no God but God." They were told to be optimistic because they were, "heading for a deed that God loves and will accept. This is the day, God willing, you spend with the women of Paradise."

> They hasten forward to Hell Fire, and mistake it for light.
>
> *Bahá'u'lláh*

Initially, the horror was diminished somewhat by the notion that this was merely a small group of crazed fanatics, but the disturbing scenes of jubilant crowds celebrating the death and destruction and gleefully brandishing photographs of terrorist leaders as if they were heroes, dashed this ray of hope. Yes there may have been an emotional high as feelings of revenge, frustration, rage and envy gave way to schadenfreude, but those duped into seeing this as a victory, will inevitably awaken to the reality that terrorism and fanaticism demand a high price. This deranged suicidal cult, devoid of conscience and bent on murder and destruction, has done incalculable damage to humanity in general, and to those whom they claim to champion in particular.

There is a finite productive capacity in the world, and after the events of September 11 a significant portion of the world's limited resources were diverted away from productive pursuits and into measures to protect against an array of potential terrorist threats. Some economists have labelled this the "fear tax" or the "terror tax". In the private sector, insurance premiums and security costs have skyrocketed, while business and consumer confidence have plummeted. Consequently, millions of people worldwide have lost their jobs, causing tax revenues to plunge. Governments confronted with higher military, security and intelligence expenditures are now faced with fewer financial resources for developmental and humanitarian aid, health care, medical research, education, and a long list of vital social needs.

Unfortunately, in our global economy, those who will suffer most are the poorest and most vulnerable, and many of them are Muslims. Now it may prove to be more difficult to come to their aid because the activities of legitimate Islamic relief organisations have been hampered, after it was alleged that some Islamic charities have funnelled relief funds to terrorists. Likewise, the livelihoods of ordinary Muslims have also been affected. For example, tourism is an important source of income for many Islamic countries, and while the travel industry worldwide has suffered, Islamic countries have been particularly hard hit. Similarly, imagine the impact the events of September 11 will have on corporate decisions about where to build future factories and assembly plants. A risk analysis for a nation with even a small number of Islamic extremists will persuade many corporations to locate elsewhere.

Currently, just as many Westerners associate Islamic countries with danger, Muslims themselves are frequently viewed with apprehension and suspicion in the West. While they may not face the same risks which the Westerners do abroad, the employment prospects and quality of life, for millions of decent and honourable Muslims living in the West, have undeniably deteriorated since the events of September 11 One can also imagine that repressive regimes in some Islamic nations will use this as a pretext to continue to deny political freedom and further curb press freedoms. Moreover, if the Western powers perceive "the street" in certain Islamic countries to be extremist, there will be little incentive for them to pressure such states to become more democratic. Lastly, many unfair and derogatory Western stereotypes about Muslims have been confirmed in the eyes of the uninformed, by the acts of those who claim to be waging "jihad" against the "infidels".

This is a dark and virulent strain of fanaticism which is bred in a culture of hate. Its leaders have failed to achieve any of their stated goals. Quite the opposite, they have profaned their religion, provoked their self-proclaimed enemies into becoming militarily stronger, and distracted governments worldwide from addressing pressing humanitarian, social, and environmental concerns. Moreover, the threat of terrorism has had a detrimental impact on personal freedom and civil liberties in nations around the world. Motivated by their lust for self-aggrandisement, terrorist leaders and extremist clerics have exploited people's frustrations and incited fanatical hatred, unperturbed by the inevitable consequences for the masses. This is nothing new, one hundred and twenty-five years ago 'Abdu'l-Bahá warned of the willingness of such clerics to manipulate the masses:

> To maintain his own leadership, he will everlastingly direct
> the masses toward that prejudice and fanaticism which subvert
> the very base of civilisation.[1]

Fortunately, after the events of September 11, 2001, we also witnessed the power of God, as people with loving hearts worldwide united as never before to come to the aid of the victims. Even in Iran, against the wishes of fanatical hardliners, young people spontaneously took to the streets to demonstrate their solidarity with the American people. Not only are the American people more united than ever before, but the democratic nations of the world have also displayed an unprecedented unity after assessing the scope of this terrorist threat. Those who would divide humanity in the name of God, have actually fused the citizens of the world closer together. As a Bahá'í, I see this as one aspect of a gradual and far-reaching process which, while at times turbulent and painful, will inevitably result in humanity recognising the need for genuine global unity. Not globalisation merely for the sake of a more efficient utilisation of human and natural resources, but a global unity which respects and celebrates human diversity, protects the planet's fragile ecology, and sets a priority on the establishment of social justice and universal peace.

Still, in our current circumstances we must guard against the danger of allowing extremists to polarise humanity. It is especially important not to confuse misguided militant extremism with the faith of Islam, even when large angry mobs identify themselves with extremism in public demonstrations. In *Surah* II of the *Qu'rán*, revealed nearly 1,400 years ago, the essence of Muhammad's revelation is expressed in a single statement. True religion is not about obscure theology, doctrine, or affiliation, it consists of belief in God and doing what is right.

> Verily, whether it be of those who believe, or those who are
> Jews or Christians or Sabaeans, whosoever believe in God and

the last day and act aright, they have their reward at their Lord's hand, and there is no fear for them, nor shall they grieve.[2]

People of all faiths, including Muslims, mourned the victims of these attacks, but true Muslims were also troubled to see their faith, founded upon tolerance and good works, defamed by hardhearted fanatics and their misguided sympathisers. In the very same *Surah*, there is another passage which, although it was revealed for a different group, is eerily suitable for today's terrorists:

> And there are those among men who say, 'We believe in God and in the last day;' but they do not believe. They would deceive God and those who do believe; but they deceive only themselves and they do not perceive. In their hearts is a sickness, and God has made them still more sick, and for them is grievous woe because they lied. And when it is said to them, 'Do not evil in the earth,' they say, 'We do but what is right.' Are not they the evildoers? and yet they do not perceive. And when it is said to them, 'Believe as other men believe,' they say, 'Shall we believe as fools believe?' Are not they themselves the fools? and yet they do not know. And when they meet those who believe, they say, 'We do believe;' but when they go aside with their devils, they say, 'We are with you; we were but mocking!' God shall mock at them and let them go on in their rebellion, blindly wandering on. Those who buy error for guidance, their traffic profits not, and they are not guided. Their likeness is as the likeness of one who kindles a fire; and when it lights up all around, God goes off with their light, and leaves them in darkness that they cannot see. Deafness, dumbness, blindness, and they shall not return![3]

Today this sickness of the heart is especially ominous because children are particularly susceptible to it. In various parts of the world, extremists have filled a void in education by establishing schools which indoctrinate children with a misrepresentation of Islam which is militant, bigoted and fanatical. Suicidal mass murder is portrayed to impressionable young minds as the holiest of acts, and those who commit murder are promised paradise and a place of honour in the hearts of true believers. Hatred is openly preached in the name of God, and prayers are followed by chants of death. Once such hatred and prejudice have taken hold, they are reinforced by a sometimes immoderate press. For example, in December of 2001 this comment appeared on the editorial page of *The Nation*, one of Pakistan's major newspapers: "The Christian world has not accepted us [Muslims] as human beings even. These nations are determined to exterminate the Muslims."

Western heads of state seek to reassure their citizens by correctly pointing out that Islam is tolerant and compassionate, and they emphasise that the vast majority of Muslims reject militancy and extremism. Lamentably, humanity still faces a clear and present danger. Keep in mind that even if only one per cent of those who profess themselves to be Muslims could be considered extremists, that would be around ten million people. If only one in a hundred of the extremists is lured to terrorism in the name of jihad, the world is faced with the daunting possibility of 100,000 would-be mass murderers. If that seems like an inflated number, consider this—European intelligence agencies estimate that approximately 70,000 men have trained in Al Qaeda terrorist camps and now live in sixty different countries. They possess financial resources estimated to be between one and five billion U.S. dollars. This means there is a real and disturbing possibility that suicidal fanatics may acquire weapons of mass destruction.[4]

Education, social justice, and the resolution of international conflicts will lessen the likelihood of terrorism in the future, but it is clear that governments must now actively hinder terrorists and dismantle their networks. Understandably, the free democracies of the world are employing various tools such as diplomacy, intelligence, surveillance, finance, humanitarian aid, and directed military action to stay the forces of terrorism. However, the long-term solution requires the use of spiritual means.

Beginning in the middle of the 19th century, Bahá'u'lláh, the founder of the Bahá'í Faith, warned mankind in unmistakable language of an impending calamity which would cause, "the limbs of mankind to quake." Some of its root causes were identified as religious fanaticism in the Middle East, and pernicious materialism in the West. Freedom was identified as a contributing factor in both instances. At first glance this seems paradoxical, but with respect to freedom, humanity has ignored the principle of moderation, a concept at the core of all religious traditions. In the West where freedom is taken to the extreme, children grow up in an environment in which virtue is derided, gratuitous violence is glorified, promiscuity is common, materialism is rampant, fashion is exploitative and degrading, and escapism, ranging from entertainment to drug abuse, is widespread. In the Middle East, the extreme repression of freedom has produced a culture which is susceptible to backwardness, intolerance, bigotry, and fanaticism. 'Abdu'l-Bahá warned long ago of this danger:

> One of the forms of prejudice which afflict the world of mankind is religious bigotry and fanaticism. When this hatred burns in human hearts, it becomes the cause of revolution, destruction, abasement of humankind and deprivation of the mercy of God... These prejudices are more pronounced in the Orient, where freedom is restricted. [5]
>
> *'Abdu'l-Bahá*

Although Bahá'ís have not known the exact nature of the calamity facing humanity, they have known for many decades that America would be whisked into its vortex once it ensued:

> It is this same cancerous materialism, born originally in Europe, carried to excess in the North American continent, contaminating the Asiatic peoples and nations, spreading its

ominous tentacles to the borders of Africa, and now invading
its very heart, which Bahá'u'lláh in unequivocal and emphatic
language denounced in His Writings, comparing it to a
devouring flame and regarding it as the chief factor in
precipitating the dire ordeals and world-shaking crises that
must necessarily involve the burning of cities and the spread
of terror and consternation in the hearts of men.[6]

Shoghi Effendi

This modern age, enshrouded in the dross of unbridled
materialism and assailed by fanatical hatred, has been offered a
fresh prescription for its ills. The essence of this healing message
is that mankind must recognise and accept the unity of the entire
human race, and grasp that all religions are but facets of a single
universal faith which derives its power from a single Creator. In
the mid-nineteenth century, the founder of the Bahá'í Faith
directed this message not only at individuals, but at their
representatives and religious leaders as well:

> O ye the elected representatives of the people in every land!
> Take ye counsel together, and let your concern be only for
> that which profiteth mankind, and bettereth the condition
> thereof, if ye be of them that scan heedfully. Regard the world
> as the human body which, though at its creation whole and
> perfect, hath been afflicted, through various causes, with grave
> disorders and maladies.[7]

> The fundamental purpose animating the Faith of God and
> His Religion is to safeguard the interests and promote the
> unity of the human race, and to foster the spirit of love and
> fellowship amongst men. Suffer it not to become a source of
> dissension and discord, of hate and enmity... Our hope is that
> the world's religious leaders and the rulers thereof will unitedly
> arise for the reformation of this age and the rehabilitation of
> its fortunes. Let them, after meditating on its needs, take
> counsel together and, through anxious and full deliberation,
> administer to a diseased and sorely-afflicted world the remedy
> it requireth...[8]

> The All-Knowing Physician hath His finger on the pulse of mankind. He perceiveth the disease, and prescribeth, in His unerring wisdom, the remedy... We can well perceive how the whole human race is encompassed with great, with incalculable afflictions. We see it languishing on its bed of sickness, sore-tried and disillusioned.
>
> The whole of mankind is in the grip of manifold ills. Strive, therefore, to save its life through the wholesome medicine which the almighty hand of the unerring Physician hath prepared.[9]
>
> *Bahá'u'lláh*

Humanity finds itself engaged in a colossal struggle against terrorism, a spiritual disease which is not unlike a malignant tumour. The democracies are united in an operation to eradicate the primary tumour, but its terrorist cells are spreading and debilitating the body of mankind with hatred, enmity, bigotry, and violence. After the tumour has been removed, treatments need to be administered to the body of mankind to successfully eradicate this disease. These treatments must be universally administered and require a therapeutic regime based upon education, and the introduction into public policy of justice, unity, and compassion.

This book deals with the diagnosis and treatment of this affliction from a Bahá'í standpoint. It deviates from the politically correct notion that the key to solving our problems lies in the peaceful but insulated coexistence of thousands of different branches and denominations of the world's religions. Although these are very troubling times, I remain optimistic because I have witnessed first-hand that there is a real and viable way for people to unite in faith without turning their backs on their respective religions. That may seem contradictory, but this is a fundamental aspect of the Bahá'í Faith which was expressed by Shoghi Effendi in this way:

The Faith standing identified with the name of Bahá'u'lláh disclaims any intention to belittle any of the Prophets gone before Him, to whittle down any of their teachings, to obscure, however slightly, the radiance of their Revelation, to oust them from the hearts of their followers, to abrogate the fundamentals of their doctrines, to discard any of their revealed Books, or to suppress the legitimate aspirations of their adherents. Repudiating the claim of any religion to be the final revelation of God to man, disclaiming finality for His own Revelation, Bahá'u'lláh inculcated the basic principle of the relativity of religious truth, the continuity of Divine Revelation, the progressiveness of religious experience. His aim is to widen the basis of all revealed religions and to unravel the mysteries of their scriptures. He insists on the unqualified recognition of the unity of their purpose, restates the eternal verities they enshrine, coordinated their functions, distinguishes the essential and the authentic from the non-essential and spurious in their teachings, separates the God-given truths from the priest-prompted superstitions, and on this as a basis proclaims the possibility, and even prophesies the inevitability, of their unification, and the consummation of their highest hopes...[10]

Over the years I have had the good fortune to meet Bahá'ís who came from Buddhist, Christian, Hindu, Jain, Jewish, Mormon, Muslim, Sikh, Shinto, and Zoroastrian backgrounds. A particularly eventful experience was the second Bahá'í World Congress, held in New York City in late November 1992. It drew more than 30,000 Bahá'ís from over 170 countries who gathered in New York to mark the 100th anniversary of the passing of Bahá'u'lláh, the founder of the Bahá'í Faith. Because attendance was limited to 30,000 participants, regional conferences were organised in Bucharest, Buenos Aires, Moscow, Nairobi, New Delhi, Panama City, Samoa, Singapore and Sydney and linked to New York via satellite. The attendees were welcomed by the Mayor of New York City and listened to a score of congratulatory messages from various dignitaries, including the President of the United States and the Governor of New York State. It was tangible proof that in just over 100 years, the Bahá'í Fáith has become the second most widespread of the independent world religions.

During one of the breaks, I wanted to meet some Arabic speaking Bahá'ís so I could ask a few questions about the literary style of Arabic found in the Bahá'í writings. As I checked the name tags, I eventually met a Palestinian Bahá'í from the West Bank. He had been raised as a Muslim and was having lunch with another Bahá'í, who, as it turned out, had been raised as a Jew. Fortunately for me, both of them spoke English and we had a most interesting conversation. Despite our Muslim, Jewish and Christian backgrounds, we were united in faith, without rejecting or belying our religious heritage. This was a microcosm of what the world could be, one I often think of when confronted with scenes of violence in the Middle East.

One of the messages of this book is that Christianity, Judaism and Islam are points on a continuum of truth. Fanatics deny that basic truth, believing that other faiths are either false or incomplete. They fail to recognise that all people are children of God, equally deserving, and equally loved by their Creator. Obviously, fanaticism is a phenomenon which can affect all religions. However, at this particular point in time, a highly militant form of global extremism, dedicated to jihad, represents the most serious risk to world peace. Therefore, much of this book deals with the relationship of Muslims, Jews, and Christians to one another. For that reason, the resulting lack of attention paid to other faiths should not be seen as a malicious omission. Also, please keep in mind that this is the work of an individual Bahá'í and it *should not* be seen as an official Bahá'í response to the question of fanaticism or terrorism. Additionally, it should be pointed out that some of my personal opinions may not reflect the views of the Bahá'í community.

These are simply the observations of a fellow traveller aboard this tiny blue world, which is racing through the vastness of space. Each of us is shaped by our unique personal experience, so rather than claiming to possess the objective truth, the best I can do is to seek to describe reality as I perceive it. In the interests of disclosure, I happened to be born in the United States, but as a young man I made a conscious decision to live in Europe. Thus, for most of my adult life I have seen the United States from afar, primarily as reported through the eyes of another culture, and I suspect that as a result I see my country more objectively than would otherwise be the case. Additionally, gradual changes are often subtle and imperceptible, but visiting America at regular intervals has allowed me to perceive changes which I otherwise would have overlooked. I liken it to looking in the mirror only once a year. With respect to religion, I happened to be born into a Christian family and raised as a Christian, but again as a young man I made a conscious decision to accept the teachings of the Bahá'í Faith. My belief in Jesus Christ never waned as a Bahá'í, quite the contrary, but because I also embraced the truth of the *Qur'án, Torah, Bhagavad-Gita*, and the teachings of Buddha, this has allowed me to see Christianity in a much broader context.

Finally, travel has assuredly affected the way I perceive the world. St. Augustine said, "the world is a book, and those who do not travel, read only one page." As a Bahá'í I have been welcomed into the homes of ordinary Bahá'ís around the world. Nearest to my heart are the villagers I have met, be the islanders in Samoa or Thailand, or desert dwellers in Rajasthan, or Navajos in the western United States. Through their simple virtue, I witnessed the oneness of humanity. They confirmed for me that the barriers which are at the root of fanaticism, such as nationality, ethnicity, race, religion, and political affiliation, are merely illusions which exist in our minds, but have no real importance in the grand scheme of things.

1
The Warning

"The Divine Messengers have been sent down, and their Books were revealed, for the purpose of promoting the knowledge of God, and of furthering unity and fellowship amongst men. But now behold, how they have made the Law of God a cause and pretext for perversity and hatred."[11]

"Religious fanaticism and hatred are a world-devouring fire, whose violence none can quench. The Hand of Divine power can, alone, deliver mankind from this desolating affliction."[12]

Bahá'u'lláh

2
Martyrs

Fanaticism turns the world on its head, it transforms the healing prescription of a messenger of God into noxious poison. When this distortion of religion is taken to the extreme, suicidal murderers are venerated as martyrs. The world of these fanatics is so dark they are unable to see the injustice of their acts. They are blinded by rage, consumed by hatred, and driven by revenge. The customary farewell per video tape, in which the killer is awash in weapons and clad in commando garb, is a pitiful attempt to attain an honoured place in this world. One can only shudder in the realisation that they actually believe the malicious and random killing of innocent non-combatants will be rewarded by God. The sad reality, plainly documented in *Surah* IV of the *Qur'án*, is that such misguided actions lead only to death, both in body and in spirit:

> And do not kill yourselves; verily, God is compassionate unto you. But whoso does that maliciously and unjustly, we will broil him with fire; for that is easy with God.

Heaven and hell, from a Bahá'í perspective, can be thought of as a similitude for a person's spiritual state, they do not represent a physical place. In life as in death, the highest and most blissful condition is nearness to God, while the most abject condition is remoteness from God. Muhammad's promise of a reward of seventy virgins, or the threat of punishment by fire were used to transform bloodthirsty tribes in seventh century Arabia into a civilised and virtuous society. He used metaphors which His listeners could understand to explain the consequences of their actions. Today we seem to be back where He started, we have to find the appropriate language to turn bloodthirsty groups into peaceful citizens of a global society.

Obviously it is easy to label these suicide murderers and their supporters as evil, but that does little to overcome the problem with which we are faced. How can we comprehend such a gruesome phenomenon? To help, let us imagine an eleven-year-old boy in Lebanon, the son of a suicide bomber. The centre of his childhood is his father, whom he is raised to revere as a "holy martyr". He knows his father primarily from his farewell video tape and the living room shrine of photos and mementoes dedicated to his father's brave "sacrifice". No thought is given to the victims, whom he was raised to consider as ruthless oppressors and infidels. In school he is treated with special respect by his teachers as the son of a "martyr", and the "glorious sacrifice" of his father is praised by his teachers to his classmates. When shopping or in the mosque he is afforded special treatment. The organisation to which his father belonged, supports his family financially so that they are the envy of the neighbourhood. His higher education will also be paid by the organisation. He also has two other uncles who are "martyrs". His grandparents are immensely proud that their sons achieved martyrdom, for they believe their sons brought glory upon the entire family, not only in this life, but in the afterlife as well.

His mother too is extremely proud of her martyred husband and enjoys the same respect in the community as her son. She proudly tells others, in her son's presence, that she hopes her son will attain martyrdom like his father. The religious leaders do everything possible to elevate the station of the suicide bombers and their families, for this is the best insurance that others will follow the same path. They go to great lengths to construct convoluted theological arguments which elevate terrorism and the killing of innocents to the level of martyrdom, even though the injunctions in the *Qur'án* against killing innocent non-combatants in an unprovoked attack are clear. Not surprisingly, their religious instruction revolves around the cult of the martyr and the struggle against subjugation. For this purpose, they misuse the history of the Imám Husayn to incite a deep and sorrowful reaction to his genuine martyrdom and then blend their suicide campaign into a seamless reaction to injustice and oppression.

Briefly, the Imám Husayn was Muhammad's grandson and rightful heir, and his plight at the hands of Muslims is indeed highly moving. Historian Edward Gibbon wrote, "In a distant age and climate, the tragic scene of the death of Hosein will awaken the sympathy of the coldest readers."[13] Husayn and his party, including many women and children, were trapped in the desert without access to water by a tyrannical group which had usurped the leadership of the Muslim community. Husayn tried to negotiate a peaceful solution, but was given an ultimatum of acknowledging the legitimacy of the usurpers, or being taken prisoner and then misused by them. Driven by conviction he could not submit to extortion, so he accepted his fate. He willingly sacrificed his life, but pleaded with his murderers to not harm the women and children in his party. His killers, however, had no qualms about killing the innocent – nor do suicide bombers. Thus it is a tragic irony that his martyrdom is used by today's suicide bombers to justify their cause. The Hizbollah leadership actually argue with a straight face that Gandhi too followed the same path of struggle as the suicide bombers, or "martyrs" as they refer to them. The implication that Husayn or Gandhi would have sanctioned the killings of women and children is simply preposterous and offensive.

Under such influences, we need not be surprised that when our eleven-year-old reached his twenties he strapped on a bomb to follow in his father's incendiary footsteps. Was he evil, or was he a victim? That is obviously a judgment for God, but as Bahá'ís we are taught that eventually each individual must accept responsibility for his own actions. In the Bahá'í writings we are taught, "God will ask everyone of his understanding and not of his following in the footsteps of others."[14] Let us not forget that as he walked among his victims and looked into their faces he made a conscious decision to kill them.

In any case, we can try to imagine the suicidal bomber's spiritual state after blowing up himself and a score of innocent bystanders. Due to his warped upbringing and distorted religious education we can assume that his intentions were actually good, even if his acts were horrifically evil. Be that as it may, suddenly he will find himself confronted with the pain and anguish of the families of his victims, orphaned children, maimed and disfigured survivors, the devastated widows and on and on. He will experience the pain and suffering which his act caused, understand the loss of the lives he cut short, and grasp the damage his acts did to the image of his religion in the eyes of the world.

Confronted with such pain and suffering and aware of how gravely he violated the true laws of God, one imagines that he would be overcome with shame and utterly unable to seek out the presence of God. He would exist with a full understanding of the extent of his evil deeds, not only to those directly touched, but also the pain and suffering of family, friends, and acquaintances. This is a hell from which there is no easy escape, save through the grace of God. Moreover, those religious leaders, teachers, and journalists who sow the seeds of such hate and enmity will also be made aware of the consequences of their deeds. It might not be the broiling fire which Muhammad promised, but it is certainly a dreadful abyss which is no less frightening.

It is a doubtless truth that poverty, repression, and political frustration are fertile soil for those who plant the seeds of hate and bigotry. Suicide killers and many of today's terrorists, however, are driven by fanatical hatred and a pathological obsession with martyrdom. Some enjoyed a comfortable life, studied abroad, and even had a promising future. So while we should strive to bring about social justice in the world and solve the various clash points in international relations, we must not overlook that the eradication of terrorism is predicated on the elimination of fanatical hatred and bigotry. Significant numbers of people are being indoctrinated into a murder and suicide cult which conditions its adherents to hate, kill and die in the name of God. They experience a sense of belonging and this, along with their "sacrifice" for the "group", gives their troubled lives meaning. This sort of fanaticism is a genuine threat to humanity, which leaders of religion and people of faith are called upon to address. A good place to start is for the Muslims, Christians, and Jews to re-examine their relationships to each other, and to begin to see their own faith through the eyes of the followers of the other faiths.

The true martyrs of religious history were guided by love, motivated by truth, and dedicated to spreading the light of God's love in a hostile world. The historian Edward Gibbon, mentioned above, estimated that some 2,000 Christians died during waves of persecution in the Roman Empire. Those brave souls sacrificed their lives to illustrate to a populace of hedonistic polytheists, the power of their faith in God. They could have escaped a cruel death simply by integrating pagan gods into their Christian beliefs and serving in the Roman army. Instead, these martyrs chose to let the light of their spirits, reflecting God's love, illumine a dark and evil world.

When Muhammad began to preach to the polytheists of Mecca, many of the first converts to Islam were poor and underprivileged. Their lack of social status afforded them little protection, thus they were often persecuted and sometimes martyred because they defied the Qureysh and refused to worship their 360 idols. They too willingly died to radiate the light of God's love in a dark, violent, and unbelieving world. It is worth mentioning that those who escaped Mecca with their lives, were given sanctuary by a benevolent Christian king in a neighbouring land. Also during the early stages of Islam when the community was in grave peril, brave souls fought against overwhelming odds to protect the lives of their fellow believers and earned the title of martyr.

In nineteenth century Persia, 20,000 luminous souls sacrificed their lives to once again shine the light of God's love among a backward, bigoted, and fanatical populace. Similarly, these martyrs could have escaped torture and a ghastly death simply by recanting their faith, but they elected instead to demonstrate the power of the holy spirit. The tremendous spiritual resolve of these brave souls was occasionally witnessed by independent observers and reported in European newspapers of the day. Thus, in an ironic twist of fate, their fanatical tormentors were unwittingly responsible for spreading the light of the Bahá'í message beyond Persia. The following account, written in the nineteenth century by an Austrian military attaché, is an example of the killing and persecution encouraged by the Islamic clerics and sanctioned by the Persian government:

From the Austrian officer, Captain von Goumoens in a letter to friends dated October 17, 1852

But follow me, my friend, you who lay claim to a heart and European ethics, follow me to the unhappy ones who, with gouged-out eyes must eat, on the scene of the deed, without any sauce, their own amputated ears; or whose teeth are torn out with inhuman violence by the hand of the executioner; or whose bare skulls are simply crushed by blows from a hammer; or where the bazar is illuminated with unhappy victims, because on right and left the people dig deep holes in their breasts and shoulders and insert burning wicks in the wounds. I saw some dragged in chains through the bazar, preceded by a military band, in whom these wicks had burned so deep that now the fat flickered convulsively in the wounds like a newly-extinguished lamp. Not seldom it happens that the unwearying ingenuity of the Orientals leads to fresh tortures. They will skin the soles of the Bábí's feet, soak the wound in boiling oil, shoe the foot like the hoof of a horse, and compel the victim to run. No cry escapes from the victim's breast; the torment is endured in dark silence by the numbed sensation of the fanatic; now he must run; the body cannot endure what the soul has endured; he falls. Give him the *coup de grace*! Put him out of his pain! No! The executioner swings the whip, and—I myself have had to witness it—the unhappy victim of hundred-fold tortures runs! This is the beginning of the end. As for the end itself, they hang the scorched and perforated bodies by their hands and feet to a tree head downwards, and now every Persian may try his marksmanship to his heart's content from a fixed but not too proximate distance on the noble quarry placed at his disposal. I saw corpses torn by nearly 150 bullets... At present I never leave my house, in order not to meet with fresh scenes of horror. After their death the Bábís are hacked in two and either nailed to the city gate, or cast out into the plain as food for the dogs and jackals.... Since my whole soul revolts against such infamy, against such abominations as recent times, according to the judgement of all, present, I will no longer maintain my connection with the scene of such crimes. [15]

What tremendous courage these Christian, Muslim and Bahá'í martyrs displayed. Unfortunately, the misuse of the term martyr when applied to suicidal killers has diminished the public's appreciation of the debt owed to the true martyrs of religious history. When we reflect, it is clear that the appearance of a Prophet would be senseless if His message were not embraced by brave souls willing to risk everything to spread it. We should not forget that the light of God's guidance has been passed on to us through of the courage and fortitude of martyrs. Remarkably, each time religion was renewed, it not only survived, but even flourished in the most oppressive and threatening of circumstances. This clearly results from the galvanising energy which attends the unveiling of God's power through a Prophet. Bahá'u'lláh revealed that this release of power transforms the world, and in the case of Jesus, He wrote:

> Know thou that when the Son of Man yielded up His breath to God, the whole creation wept with a great weeping. By sacrificing Himself, however, a fresh capacity was infused into all created things. Its evidences, as witnessed in all the peoples of the earth, are now manifest before thee. The deepest wisdom which the sages have uttered, the profoundest learning which any mind hath unfolded, the arts which the ablest hands have produced, the influence exerted by the most potent of rulers, are but manifestations of the quickening power released by His transcendent, His all-pervasive, and resplendent Spirit.

> We testify that when He came into the world, He shed the splendor of His glory upon all created things. Through Him the leper recovered from the leprosy of perversity and ignorance. Through Him, the unchaste and wayward were healed. Through His power, born of Almighty God, the eyes of the blind were opened, and the soul of the sinner sanctified.

> Leprosy may be interpreted as any veil that interveneth between man and the recognition of the Lord, his God.

Whoso alloweth himself to be shut out from Him is indeed a leper, who shall not be remembered in the Kingdom of God, the Mighty, the All-Praised. We bear witness that through the power of the Word of God every leper was cleansed, every sickness was healed, every human infirmity was banished. He it is Who purified the world. Blessed is the man who, with a face beaming with light, hath turned towards Him.[16]

Bahá'u'lláh

Clearly, when the Light of God breaks among the most backward people during the darkest of times, these luminous souls are the clearest proof of the power of God's word. Shoghi Effendi stressed this as the principal reason for the Bahá'í Faith being revealed among the Muslims of Persia:

...it should always be borne in mind, nor can it be sufficiently emphasized, that the primary reason why the Báb and Bahá'u'lláh chose to appear in Persia, and to make it the first repository of their Revelation, was because, of all the peoples and nations of the civilized world, that race and nation had, as so often depicted by 'Abdu'l-Bahá, sunk to such ignominious depths, and manifested so great a perversity, as to find no parallel among its contemporaries. For no more convincing proof could be adduced demonstrating the regenerating spirit animating the Revelations proclaimed by the Báb and Bahá'u'lláh than their power to transform what can be truly regarded as one of the most backward, the most cowardly, and perverse of peoples into a race of heroes, fit to effect in turn a similar revolution in the life of mankind. [17]

Shoghi Effendi

In the nineteenth century, a young Orientalist, Professor Edward G. Browne of Cambridge University, began studying the Bábi/ Bahá'í phenomenon after reports from Persia began to reach

Europe. He corroborated the remarkable transforming power of this new faith and encouraged others to undertake its study as the following extract from his writings attests:

> Now it appears to me that the history of the Bábi movement must be interesting in different ways to others besides those who are directly engaged in the study of Persian. To the student of religious thought it will afford no little matter for reflection; for here he may contemplate such personalities as by lapse of time pass into heroes and demi-gods still unobscured by myth and fable; he may examine by the light of concurrent and independent testimony one of those strange outbursts of enthusiasm, faith, fervent devotion, and indomitable heroism...which we are accustomed to associate with the earlier history of the human race; he may witness, in a word, the birth of a faith which may not impossibly win a place amidst the great religions of the world. To the ethnologist also it may yield food for thought as to the character of a people who, stigmatised as they often have been as selfish, mercenary, avaricious, egotistical, sordid, and cowardly, are yet capable of exhibiting under the influence of a strong religious impulse a degree of devotion, disinterestedness, generosity, unselfishness, nobility, and courage which may be paralleled in history, but can scarcely be surpassed. [18]

3
Spiritual Leaders

As is the case with the term "martyr", the designation "spiritual leader" is sometimes erroneously applied to fanatics driven by hatred and vengeance, whose diatribes incite malice and enmity in the hearts of their followers. As 'Abdu'l-Bahá taught, those who habitually preach hatred are not spiritual leaders:

> The foundations of the divine religions are one... Whosoever is lacking in love for humanity or manifests hatred and bigotry toward any part of it violates the foundation and source of his own belief... [19]

A spiritual leader is a teacher of divine truths. Such a teacher instructs his or her followers that for every question or problem, there is a spiritual answer or solution. Spiritual solutions bring peace and progress, these universal answers are the revealed word of God found in teachings of all religions.

> The purpose of religion as revealed from the heaven of God's holy Will is to establish unity and concord amongst the peoples of the world; make it not the cause of dissension and strife. The religion of God and His divine law are the most potent instruments and the surest of all means for the dawning of the light of unity amongst men. The progress of the world, the development of nations, the tranquillity of peoples, and the peace of all who dwell on earth are among the principles and ordinances of God.

> Religion bestoweth upon man the most precious of all gifts, offereth the cup of prosperity, imparteth eternal life, and showereth imperishable benefits upon mankind.[20]
>
> *Bahá'u'lláh*

Like many beneficial institutions and mechanisms, religion can become dangerous when it falls into the hands of fanatics:

> Our purpose is to show how true religion promotes the civilisation and honor, the prosperity and prestige, the learning and advancement of a people once abject, enslaved and ignorant, and how, when it falls into the hands of religious leaders who are foolish and fanatical, it is diverted to the wrong ends, until this greatest of splendors turns into blackest night.[21]
>
> *'Abdu'l-Bahá*

A religious leader can become a fanatic, or a fanatic can become a religious leader, but a fanatical religious leader can never be a spiritual leader. There is a simple unambiguous spiritual reaction to those who preach hatred:

> Religion should unite all hearts and cause wars and disputes to vanish from the face of the earth, give birth to spirituality, and bring life and light to each heart. If religion becomes a cause of dislike, hatred and division, it were better to be without it, and to withdraw from such a religion would be a truly religious act. For it is clear that the purpose of a remedy is to cure; but if the remedy should only aggravate the complaint it had better be left alone. Any religion which is not a cause of love and unity is no religion. All the holy prophets were as doctors to the soul; they gave prescriptions for the healing of mankind; thus any remedy that causes disease does not come from the great and supreme Physician.
>
> *'Abdu'l-Bahá*

This does not mean that spiritual leaders cannot point out injustice, or warn of the culture or aims of another nation. It is understandable, for example, that some religious leaders might disagree with the foreign policy of a particular government, distrust its motives, and harbour resentment for past actions. It is reasonable that some would feel threatened by a culture which frequently undermines the values shared by all the world's religions, and whose mass entertainment glorifies violence and moral laxity. One can accept that a "spiritual leader" might disapprove of America's corrupting materialism, and seek to limit its influence by warning of its dangers. Indeed, one could even view this as a spiritual duty, the product of love and genuine concern. Such warnings, however, are not sweeping condemnations of millions of people, nor are they designed to incite violence or induce hatred.

In contrast, the fanatic is not motivated by love for humanity. In the name of God he assails an entire people, plants seeds of hate in the susceptible hearts of others, and waters them with torrents of rage. In extreme cases, children grow up hearing their prayers followed by chants of, "death to America", or, "death to Israel." This extreme bigotry results in a mindset which makes it easy to kill innocent unknowns whom the fanatic considers his mortal enemies. In his mind they bear responsibility for any and all injustices, real or perceived.

The fanatical leader further envenoms his followers by instilling in them, a victimisation mentality, which reinforces a cycle of violence. A spiritual leader encourages forgiveness, but a fanatical leader shuns forgiveness and demands vengeance, promising paradise for avengers. An example of this misguided fervour occurred a few years ago in Luxor, Egypt. It was reported that fanatics bathed their arms in the blood of innocent European tourists and emitted cries of ecstasy as they stabbed their victims to death.

Fanatical leaders, fuelled by hatred and bigotry, are responsible for the development of a pathological mental state among their followers. This is not limited to terrorists and their immediate supporters. In communities in which fanatical leaders hold sway, truth, rational thought and objective reasoning are sacrificed in order to justify hate-based ideologies. A victimisation mentality invariably leads to a distortion of reality. Truth and logic are readily discarded in order to construct an alternative reality in which the perceived enemy is ultimately responsible for all the world's injustices. Elaborate and outlandish conspiracy theories replace truth in the mind of the fanatic.

In addition to a distortion of reality, today's jihad-inspired fanatics have distorted the true character of a faith which was intended to establish tolerance and brotherhood among mankind. Spiritual leaders don't lead chants of death after communal prayers, they teach spiritual truths:

> Shall I not inform you of a better act than fasting, alms and prayer? Making peace between one another: enmity and malice tear up heavenly rewards by the roots.[22]
>
> *Muhammad*

4
Spiritual Education

The Golden Rule, found in all religions, is universally recognised as the basis of true spiritual education. This simple statement, to treat others as we would like to be treated, is the key to ushering in humanity's Golden Age. When Jesus was asked by the Jews which is the greatest commandment, He responded by quoting from the Torah:

> Thou shalt love the Lord thy God with all thy heart, and with all thy soul, and with all thy mind. This is the first and great commandment. And the second is like unto it, Thou shalt love thy neighbour as thyself. On these two commandments hang all the law and the prophets. [23]

This brought the next question: who then is my neighbour? The implication was that neighbour refers exclusively to fellow Jews. Jesus, however, repeatedly taught that it was not particularly virtuous to love one's own kind, virtue consists of loving those outside of one's circle of family, friends and acquaintances. He used the parable of the Good Samaritan to explain His point. If we revised this parable for a Muslim child of today, it might read something like this:

> A Muslim man was on his way to Sarajevo from Belgrade when he was attacked by a gang of thieves. He was robbed, stripped of his clothes, and left half dead on the side of the road.

By chance a certain mullah came along that way, and when he saw the man, he became leery and quickly decided to pass by on the other side of the street. Later, when a finely dressed sayyid came along, he likewise averted his eyes and passed on the other side of the road.

But a certain Hindu happened to pass and out of compassion went to the man. He gave him his coat, dressed his wounds, and carried him to a small inn. He continued to look after him for the rest of the day until he was out of danger. When he departed the next day he paid the bill and gave the innkeeper 50 Euros and asked him to look after the man. He promised to take care of any additional expenses the next time he returned.

In his hour of need, of these three, who was the man's neighbour and brother in faith? Clearly it was the one who showed compassion towards him.

So go and behave like a true brother in faith! [24]

Spiritual education teaches a child to view all mankind as neighbours in a global village. It stresses love, compassion, patience and mercy for all creatures. It results in tolerance, openness, harmony, and progress. A child with a spiritual education dreams of making the world a better place. He or she will want to contribute to the advancement of civilisation by creating uplifting art, building structures which stand the test of time, pushing the limits of human knowledge, or simply serving the needs of humanity. He or she will be awed by the power and majesty of creation.

On the other hand, a fanatical religious education teaches a child to distrust those whose beliefs or appearance are different. Such a child is taught to hate and look disdainfully upon "non-believers". Taken to the extreme, the child is imbued with rage, resentment, and anger toward "non-believers", and he sees those who don't share his extreme beliefs, even within his own religion, as enemies.

The aspirations of such children are dark and destructive. They dream of strapping on bombs and walking among pedestrians, unaware of their intentions, and killing as many as possible. Such children don't dream of building great structures, they dream of death and destruction, of hijacking planes and flying them into buildings. They may learn to recite a holy book from memory, but as Jesus remarked, while they know every letter, they understand not a word.

In certain quarters, the condemnation of terrorism is accompanied with obligatory qualifying remarks about the need to address its root causes. Interestingly, they seldom identify the underlying cause of terrorism as fanatical hatred and bigotry. Granted, poverty and injustice make it easier to find reasons to hate, but it is the fostering of fanaticism, hatred, prejudice and intolerance in a repressive society which leads to terrorism.

Think back to Nazi Germany, it is self-evident that repressive societies don't allow criticism, self-determination, open debate, or freedom of expression. In order to keep internal pressure down, repressive governments encourage the media under their control to project blame upon scapegoats, the Jews in the case of Nazi Germany, and in the case of many repressive states in the 21st century, Christians and Jews. If we want to address the true causes of today's terrorism, at the top of the list must stand: repression, self-pity, fanatical hatred, bigotry, envy, resentment, misdirected anger, and a perversion of the concept of martyrdom.

The global community shares the responsibility of preventing innocent impressionable children from being brainwashed in the cause of hatred, violence and destruction. This is an integral aspect in the prevention of terrorism, and mankind's peace and security depend upon it. However, this cannot be done by politicians alone, religious leaders and people of faith must take action to prevent a corruption of shared universal values.

'Abdu'l-Bahá pointed out to Muslims the significance of spiritual education by sketching the development of the early Christians:

> Consider the wonderful effect of spiritual education and training. By it the fisherman Peter was transformed into the greatest of teachers. Spiritual education made the disciples radiant lamps in the darkness of the world and caused the Christians of the first and second centuries to become renowned everywhere for their virtues. Even philosophers bore testimony to this. Among them was Galen, the physician, who wrote a book upon the subject of the progress of the nations. He was a celebrated philosopher of the Greeks, although not a Christian. In his book he stated that religious beliefs exercise a tremendous influence upon civilisation and that the world is in need of such belief. In proof of this, he said, in substance, 'In our time there is a certain people called Christians, who, though neither philosophers nor scholastically trained, are superior to all others as regards their morality. They are perfect in morals. Each one of them is like a great philosopher in morals, ethics and turning toward the Kingdom of God.' This is evidence from the testimony of an intelligent outside observer that spiritual education is the light of the world of humanity and that its absence in the world is darkness itself.
>
> *'Abdu'l-Bahá*

Ideally, children should learn the history and essence of all faiths, and gather the fruits of spiritual guidance found in all the Books of God, and see themselves and others as creatures of a single Creator.

> Schools must first train the children in the principles of religion, so that the Promise and the Threat recorded in the Books of God may prevent them from the things

forbidden and adorn them with the mantle of the
commandments; but this in such a measure that it may
not injure the children by resulting in ignorant fanaticism
and bigotry.[25]

Bahá'u'lláh

5
Spiritual Laws

The principles of religion include laws and commandments which can be categorised into two main groups. The first and most significant classification comprises the spiritual laws which are the timeless universal aspect of religion. These truths are changeless and have been reaffirmed in the message of every ensuing prophet. The other group includes religious ordinances which are primarily concerned with the practical aspects of daily life and human interaction. Topics such as rites, ceremonies, crime, punishment, personal hygiene, preparation of food, and clothing would be included in this group. Clearly, circumstances change over time, and laws, once practical, must be adapted to better serve the needs of humanity.

'Abdu'l-Bahá, speaking in Paris in 1911 of the essential harmony of science and religion, gave this explanation of the spiritual and practical aspects of religion:

> The Unity of God is logical, and this idea is not antagonistic to the conclusions arrived at by scientific study. All religions teach that we must do good, that we must be generous, sincere, truthful, law-abiding, and faithful; all this is reasonable, and logically the only way in which humanity can progress.

> All religious laws conform to reason, and are suited to the people for whom they are framed, and for the age in which they are to be obeyed.

Religion has two main parts:

1) The Spiritual.

2) The Practical.

The spiritual part never changes. All the Manifestations of God and His Prophets have taught the same truths and given the same spiritual law. They all teach the one code of morality. There is no division in the truth. The Sun has sent forth many rays to illumine human intelligence, the light is always the same.

The practical part of religion deals with exterior forms and ceremonies, and with modes of punishment for certain offences. This is the material side of the law, and guides the customs and manners of the people.

In the time of Moses, there were ten crimes punishable by death. When Christ came this was changed; the old axiom 'an eye for an eye, and a tooth for a tooth' was converted into 'Love your enemies, do good to them that hate you', the stern old law being changed into one of love, mercy and forbearance!

In the former days the punishment for theft was the cutting off of the right hand; in our time this law could not be so applied. In this age, a man who curses his father is allowed to live, when formerly he would have been put to death. It is therefore evident that whilst the spiritual law never alters, the practical rules must change their application with the necessities of the time. The spiritual aspect of religion is the greater, the more important of the two, and this is the same for all time, it never changes! It is the same, yesterday, today, and for ever! 'As it was the beginning, is now, and ever shall be.'

Now, all questions of morality contained in the spiritual, immutable law of every religion are logically right. If religion were contrary to logical reason then it would cease to be a religion and be merely a tradition. Religion and science are the two wings upon which man's intelligence can soar into the heights, with which the human soul can progress. It is not possible to fly with one wing alone! Should a man try to fly with the wing of religion alone he would quickly fall into the quagmire of superstition, whilst on the other hand, with the wing of science alone he would also make no progress, but fall into the despairing slough of materialism. All religions of the present day have fallen into superstitious practices, out of harmony alike with the true principles of the teaching they represent and with the scientific discoveries of the time. Many religious leaders have grown to think that the importance of religion lies mainly in the adherence to a collection of certain dogmas and the practice of rites and ceremonies! Those whose souls they profess to cure are taught to believe likewise, and these cling tenaciously to the outward forms, confusing them with the inward truth.

Now, these forms and rituals differ in the various churches and amongst the different sects, and even contradict one another; giving rise to discord, hatred, and disunion. The outcome of all this dissension is the belief of many cultured men that religion and science are contradictory terms, that religion needs no powers of reflection, and should in no wise be regulated by science, but must of necessity be opposed, the one to the other. The unfortunate effect of this is that science has drifted apart from religion, and religion has become a mere blind and more or less apathetic following of the precepts of certain religious teachers, who insist on their own favourite dogmas being accepted even when they are contrary to science. This is foolishness, for it is quite evident that science is the light, and, being so, religion truly so-called does not oppose knowledge.[26]

A fundamentalist is likely to equate a dogmatic adherence to tradition as an effective defence against the weakening of his beliefs. If a fundamentalist conscientiously conforms to the more important spiritual laws, he may stand in the way of progress, but he does not represent a danger to mankind's peace and security. However, when fundamentalists ignore, misrepresent, or misapprehend the higher spiritual aspect of religion, then there is a potential for danger. Herein lies the difference between fanaticism and fundamentalism, fanaticism is not tempered with genuine spirituality. Fanatics hold the essence of religion to be a tyrannical enforcement of customs intended for people who lived fourteen hundred, two thousand, or several thousand years ago.

For example, Muhammad revealed in the *Qur'án* that there was to be no compulsion in Islam, yet "orthodoxy police" have appeared in some fundamentalist societies to brutally enforce the outward aspects of religion. In other societies, fanatical vigilantes have sometimes taken responsibility into their own hands and murdered people who were seen reading a secular newspaper at a cafe, or earning a living by running a movie projector in a cinema.

'Abdu'l-Bahá explained the dangers of religious stagnation this way:

> Religion is the outer expression of the divine reality. Therefore, it must be living, vitalised, moving and progressive. If it be without motion and non-progressive, it is without the divine life; it is dead. The divine institutes are continuously active and evolutionary; therefore, the revelation of them must be progressive and continuous. All things are subject to reformation. This is a century of life and renewal. Sciences and arts, industry and invention have been reformed. Law and ethics have been reconstituted, reorganised. The world of thought has been regenerated. Sciences of former ages and philosophies of

the past are useless today. Present exigencies demand new methods of solution; world problems are without precedent. Old ideas and modes of thought are fast becoming obsolete. Ancient laws and archaic ethical systems will not meet the requirements of modern conditions, for this is clearly the century of a new life, the century of the revelation of reality and, therefore, the greatest of all centuries. Consider how the scientific developments of fifty years have surpassed and eclipsed the knowledge and achievements of all the former ages combined. Would the announcements and theories of ancient astronomers explain our present knowledge of the suns and planetary systems? Would the mask of obscurity which beclouded medieval centuries meet the demand for clear-eyed vision and understanding which characterises the world today? Will the despotism of former governments answer the call for freedom which has risen from the heart of humanity in this cycle of illumination? It is evident that no vital results are now forthcoming from the customs, institutions and standpoints of the past. In view of this, shall blind imitations of ancestral forms and theological interpretations continue to guide and control the religious life and spiritual development of humanity today? Shall man, gifted with the power of reason, unthinkingly follow and adhere to dogma, creeds and hereditary beliefs which will not bear the analysis of reason in this century of effulgent reality? Unquestionably this will not satisfy men of science, for when they find premise or conclusion contrary to present standards of proof and without real foundation, they reject that which has been formerly accepted as standard and correct and move forward from new foundations.[27]

When Christ appeared He was met with animosity because He chastised the religious leaders of His day for ignoring the spiritual dimension of their religion and rigidly focusing on customs and ordinances which grew out of intractable human interpretations of the law.

> But woe to ye Pharisees! for you tithe mint and rue and
> every herb, and neglect justice and the love of God. [28]
>
> *Jesus*

We saw in the previous section that Muhammad taught His followers that making peace was more important than fasting, giving alms, and prayer. In another section of the *Qu'rán*, He explains that righteousness is not about outward forms such as turning towards Mecca in prayer. He explains that a righteous person is one who believes in God and acts accordingly by sharing his wealth with the less fortunate, keeping his word when he gives it, and remaining unruffled in times of poverty and distress. It is important for religious people of all faiths to understand that fanaticism can be overcome by concentrating on the spiritual aspect of religion. Moreover, if children are taught the universal spiritual laws of all faiths, this will allow them to develop a spirit of tolerance and unity.

6
Spiritual Choice

People tend to be very proud of their allegiance to a particular religion and deem their belief a dramatic and courageous acceptance of truth over falsehood. In fact, most people simply adopt the religion of their parents, and if they do branch out, it will usually be to another denomination or group within the same religion.

The commingling of religion with festivals, holidays, elaborate ceremonials, traditions and music in early childhood has the advantage of instilling a deep and abiding faith. This is because such impulses are stored in a portion of the brain which is associated with emotions, territoriality and the like. The drawback is that if religion is not augmented with deepening in the holy books and genuine reflection, a person's spiritual perspective is significantly limited. Sometimes narrow-mindedness and intolerance may follow and when this happens, divergent views are quickly perceived as threatening and result in an emotional and aggressive response.

If someone is born in a Jewish community to Jewish parents and accepts Christ, that is unquestionably a difficult and valiant act. It might result in such a person being disowned and rejected by his or her own family. The same would be true for a Christian who recognises Muhammad, or a Muslim who accepts the message of Bahá'u'lláh.

Simply following the crowd and swimming with the current is not particularly eventful. The people in Christ's day who rejected Him were quite proud of their faith and allegiance to Moses. Moses was the accepted spiritual leader of the day and following Him required no particular act of courage. Only those who swam against the current placed themselves in danger. That is why Christ, Muhammad, Bahá'u'lláh, and their early followers suffered so greatly. Can those people today who are proud of their belief in Jesus or Muhammad be sure they would have had the courage and spiritual conviction to follow when it would have resulted in ostracism or persecution? Jesus warned His followers of the hatred that would befall them:

> These things I command you, that ye love one another. If the world hate you, ye know that it hated me before it hated you. If ye were of the world, the world would love his own: but because ye are not of the world, but I have chosen you out of the world, therefore the world hateth you. [29]

A Christian should search his or her conscience and answer this question: Am I certain I would be a Christian if I had been born to a Buddhist family in Sri Lanka? A Muslim might ask: Would I be a Muslim if I had been born to a Jewish family in Canada? If we take time to think it through, most of us understand that very few people could answer yes to such a question. Once we come to that realisation, then comes the next question: Since I've never truly made an objective study of other faiths, can I be certain that mine is the only correct choice?

As a Bahá'í one recognises that each believer makes a correct choice, because the choices are not mutually exclusive. If we equate religion to math and science, it would be as though one group held fast to the mathematics of Pythagoras and held all others to be in error. Yes, they would be right in claiming to follow the truth, but they would be incorrect in believing that others were in error. The next group might be followers of Kepler, the next Newton, the next Einstein and so on. To support the teachings of Newton one need not reject the mathematics of Pythagoras, on the contrary the one builds upon the other. Religion can be seen in the same way, one can assimilate the truth and wisdom of the past without compromising one's belief. Truth is thereby expanded, not negated. But to reach this conclusion one has to be willing to undertake an unfettered exploration for truth.

'Abdu'l-Bahá explained the importance of an independent search after truth this way:

> The divine Prophets have revealed and founded religion. They have laid down certain laws and heavenly principles for the guidance of mankind. They have taught and promulgated the knowledge of God, established praiseworthy ethical ideals and inculcated the highest standards of virtues in the human world. Gradually these heavenly teachings and foundations of reality have been beclouded by human interpretations and dogmatic imitations of ancestral beliefs. The essential realities, which the Prophets labored so hard to establish in human hearts and minds while undergoing ordeals and suffering tortures of persecution, have now well nigh vanished. Some of these heavenly Messengers have been killed, some imprisoned, all of Them despised and rejected while proclaiming the reality of Divinity. Soon after Their departure from this world, the essential truth of Their teachings was lost sight of and dogmatic imitations adhered to.

> Inasmuch as human interpretations and blind imitations differ widely, religious strife and disagreement have arisen among mankind, the light of true religion has been extinguished and the unity of the world of humanity destroyed. The Prophets of God voiced the spirit of unity and agreement. They have been the Founders of divine

reality. Therefore, if the nations of the world forsake imitations and investigate the reality underlying the revealed Word of God, they will agree and become reconciled. For reality is one and not multiple.

The nations and religions are steeped in blind and bigoted imitations. A man is a Jew because his father was a Jew. The Muslim follows implicitly the footsteps of his ancestors in belief and observance. The Buddhist is true to his heredity as a Buddhist. That is to say, they profess religious belief blindly and without investigation, making unity and agreement impossible. It is evident, therefore, that this condition will not be remedied without a reformation in the world of religion. In other words, the fundamental reality of the divine religions must be renewed, reformed, revoiced to mankind.

From the seed of reality religion has grown into a tree which has put forth leaves and branches, blossoms and fruit. After a time this tree has fallen into a condition of decay. The leaves and blossoms have withered and perished; the tree has become stricken and fruitless. It is not reasonable that man should hold to the old tree, claiming that its life forces are undiminished, its fruit unequaled, its existence eternal. The seed of reality must be sown again in human hearts in order that a new tree may grow therefrom and new divine fruits refresh the world. By this means the nations and peoples now divergent in religion will be brought into unity, imitations will be forsaken, and a universal brotherhood in reality itself will be established. Warfare and strife will cease among mankind; all will be reconciled as servants of God. For all are sheltered beneath the tree of His providence and mercy. God is kind to all; He is the giver of bounty to all alike, even as Jesus Christ has declared that God "sendeth rain on the just and on the unjust"—that is to say, the mercy of God is universal. All humanity is under the protection of His love and favor, and unto all He has pointed the way of guidance and progress. Progress is of two kinds: material and spiritual. The former is attained through observation of the surrounding existence and constitutes the foundation of civilization. Spiritual progress is through the breaths of the Holy Spirit and is the awakening of the conscious soul of man to perceive the reality of Divinity. Material progress ensures the happiness of the human world. Spiritual progress ensures the happiness and eternal continuance of the soul. The Prophets of God have founded the laws of divine civilization. They have been the root and fundamental source of all knowledge.

They have established the principles of human brotherhood, of fraternity, which is of various kinds—such as the fraternity of family, of race, of nation and of ethical motives. These forms of fraternity, these bonds of brotherhood, are merely temporal and transient in association. They do not ensure harmony and are usually productive of disagreement. They do not prevent warfare and strife; on the contrary, they are selfish, restricted and fruitful causes of enmity and hatred among mankind. The spiritual brotherhood which is enkindled and established through the breaths of the Holy Spirit unites nations and removes the cause of warfare and strife. It transforms mankind into one great family and establishes the foundations of the oneness of humanity. It promulgates the spirit of international agreement and ensures universal peace. Therefore, we must investigate the foundation of this heavenly fraternity. We must forsake all imitations and promote the reality of the divine teachings. In accordance with these principles and actions and by the assistance of the Holy Spirit, both material and spiritual happiness shall become realized. Until all nations and peoples become united by the bonds of the Holy Spirit in this real fraternity, until national and international prejudices are effaced in the reality of this spiritual brotherhood, true progress, prosperity and lasting happiness will not be attained by man.[30]

'Abdu'l-Bahá

7

The Other Half

If a nation discriminates against and oppresses a particular race of people, the free and democratic world is apt to react with censure, possibly even political isolation and or economic sanctions. Strangely, if a nation discriminates against and oppresses an entire gender, this is accepted in the name of religious tolerance, even though the majority of people on the planet are women.

Ironically, the most ruthless oppressors of women are often the very men who consider themselves the victims of injustice. If women are denied education, if their talents are not cultivated, and if their dreams and aspirations are frustrated, the world is deprived of a tremendous source of talent, creativity, and ingenuity. The world needs to begin to view the persecution and subjugation of women as unacceptable. However, respect for religious tolerance precludes a political or economic response to the oppression of women.

This is a pivotal reason why spiritual renewal is necessary. Those who have studied the history of Islam know that Muhammad dramatically improved the status of women in seventh century Arabia. Infanticide of girls was expressly forbidden, women were given rights of inheritance, and laws regulating divorce and the proper treatment of women were revealed. Equally important, women were promised the same spiritual rewards as men.

There are, however, passages from the *Qu'rán* which sometimes have been interpreted so as to severely restrict the rights and freedoms of women (see *Surah* IV:34). Fanatics have so grossly distorted the revelation of Muhammad that it is now used as a justification of inhumanity towards women. In the most extreme societies, women have been denied education and medical attention, and some actually suffered from vitamin D deficiency because they sat in darkened rooms and were completely covered when outdoors. In some Islamic societies, women who seek to live an independent life risk being executed by male family members who would then enjoy the respect of the family, as well as impunity from criminal prosecution.

A few years ago, the BBC broadcasted a shocking documentary of a young boy in rural Pakistan who shot and killed his own widowed mother because she continued to leave their house without a male escort. The boy was treated as a hero in his village, a protector of the honour of his faith and family. This inhumanity to women, in and of itself, is a clarion call for the necessity of a spiritual reawakening.

In the United States the constitutional amendment which gave women the right to vote was not ratified until 1920. Eight years earlier, in 1912, 'Abdu'l-Bahá visited North America and spoke often of the equality of women and emphasised the importance of women to the establishment of a true and lasting universal peace. Here is a portion of a talk he gave in Chicago:

> In this day man must investigate reality impartially and without prejudice in order to reach the true knowledge and conclusions. What, then, constitutes the inequality between man and woman? Both are human. In powers and function each is the complement of the other. At most it is this: that woman has been denied the opportunities which man has so long enjoyed, especially the privilege of education. But even this is not always a shortcoming. Shall

we consider it an imperfection and weakness in her nature that she is not proficient in the school of military tactics, that she cannot go forth to the field of battle and kill, that she is not able to handle a deadly weapon? Nay, rather, is it not a compliment when we say that in hardness of heart and cruelty she is inferior to man? The woman who is asked to arm herself and kill her fellow creatures will say, "I cannot." Is this to be considered a fault and lack of qualification as man's equal? Yet be it known that if woman had been taught and trained in the military science of slaughter, she would have been the equivalent of man even in this accomplishment. But God forbid! May woman never attain this proficiency; may she never wield weapons of war, for the destruction of humanity is not a glorious achievement. The upbuilding of a home, the bringing of joy and comfort into human hearts are truly glories of mankind. Let not a man glory in this, that he can kill his fellow creatures; nay, rather, let him glory in this, that he can love them.

When we consider the kingdoms of existence below man, we find no distinction or estimate of superiority and inferiority between male and female. Among the myriad organisms of the vegetable and animal kingdoms sex exists, but there is no differentiation whatever as to relative importance and value in the equation of life. If we investigate impartially, we may even find species in which the female is superior or preferable to the male. For instance, there are trees such as the fig, the male of which is fruitless while the female is fruitful. The male of the date palm is valueless while the female bears abundantly. Inasmuch as we find no ground for distinction or superiority according to the creative wisdom in the lower kingdoms, is it logical or becoming of man to make such distinction in regard to himself? The male of the animal kingdom does not glory in its being male and superior to the female. In fact, equality exists and is recognised. Why should man, a higher and more intelligent creature, deny and deprive himself of this equality the animals enjoy? His surest index and guide as to the creative intention concerning himself are the conditions and analogies of the kingdoms below him where equality of the sexes is fundamental.

The truth is that all mankind are the creatures and servants of one God, and in His estimate all are human. Man is a generic term applying to all humanity. The biblical statement "Let us make man in our image, after our likeness" does not mean that woman was not created. The image and likeness of God apply to her as well. In Persian and Arabic there are two distinct words translated into English as man: one meaning man and woman collectively, the other distinguishing man as male from woman the female. The first word and its pronoun are generic, collective; the other is restricted to the male. This is the same in Hebrew.

To accept and observe a distinction which God has not intended in creation is ignorance and superstition. The fact which is to be considered, however, is that woman, having formerly been deprived, must now be allowed equal opportunities with man for education and training. There must be no difference in their education. Until the reality of equality between man and woman is fully established and attained, the highest social development of mankind is not possible. Even granted that woman is inferior to man in some degree of capacity or accomplishment, this or any other distinction would continue to be productive of discord and trouble. The only remedy is education, opportunity; for equality means equal qualification. In brief, the assumption of superiority by man will continue to be depressing to the ambition of woman, as if her attainment to equality was creationally impossible; woman's aspiration toward advancement will be checked by it, and she will gradually become hopeless. On the contrary, we must declare that her capacity is equal, even greater than man's. This will inspire her with hope and ambition, and her susceptibilities for advancement will continually increase. She must not be told and taught that she is weaker and inferior in capacity and qualification. If a pupil is told that his intelligence is less than his fellow pupils, it is a very great drawback and handicap to his progress. He must be encouraged to advance by the statement, "You are most capable, and if you endeavor, you will attain the highest degree."

It is my hope that the banner of equality may be raised throughout the five continents where as yet it is not fully recognized and established. In this enlightened world of the West woman has advanced an immeasurable degree beyond the women of the Orient. And let it be known once more that until woman and man recognise and realize equality, social and political progress here or anywhere will not be possible. For the world of humanity consists of two parts or members: one is woman; the other is man. Until these two members are equal in strength, the oneness of humanity cannot be established, and the happiness and felicity of mankind will not be a reality. God willing, this is to be so.[31]

'Abdu'l-Bahá

8
Mankind's Greatest Danger

Speaking in Paris in 1911, 'Abdu'l-Bahá stressed that the peace and security of humanity is unattainable unless and until prejudice is overcome. Today, living in the European Union it is difficult to imagine that in the previous century, two wars were fought here, which went on to engulf much of the world. Millions of people perished and today the descendants of these once bitter enemies are united to a degree unthinkable as 'Abdu'l-Bahá spoke these words:

> All prejudices, whether of religion, race, politics or nation, must be renounced, for these prejudices have caused the world's sickness. It is a grave malady which, unless arrested, is capable of causing the destruction of the whole human race. Every ruinous war, with its terrible bloodshed and misery, has been caused by one or other of these prejudices.

> The deplorable wars going on in these days are caused by the fanatical religious hatred of one people for another, or the prejudices of race or colour.

> Until all these barriers erected by prejudice are swept away, it is not possible for humanity to be at peace. For this reason Bahá'u'lláh has said, 'These Prejudices are destructive to mankind'.

> Contemplate first the prejudice of religion: consider the nations of so-called religious people; if they were truly

worshippers of God they would obey His law which forbids them to kill one another.

If priests of religion really adored the God of love and served the Divine Light, they would teach their people to keep the chief Commandment, 'To be in love and charity with all men'. But we find the contrary, for it is often the priests who encourage nations to fight. Religious hatred is ever the most cruel!

All religions teach that we should love one another; that we should seek out our own shortcomings before we presume to condemn the faults of others, that we must not consider ourselves superior to our neighbours! We must be careful not to exalt ourselves lest we be humiliated.

Who are we that we should judge? How shall we know who, in the sight of God, is the most upright man? God's thoughts are not like our thoughts! How many men who have seemed saint-like to their friends have fallen into the greatest humiliation. Think of Judas Iscariot; he began well, but remember his end! On the other hand, Paul, the Apostle, was in his early life an enemy of Christ, whilst later he became His most faithful servant. How then can we flatter ourselves and despise others?

Let us therefore be humble, without prejudices, preferring others' good to our own! Let us never say, 'I am a believer but he is an infidel', 'I am near to God, whilst he is an outcast'. We can never know what will be the final judgment! Therefore let us help all who are in need of any kind of assistance.

Let us teach the ignorant, and take care of the young child until he grows to maturity. When we find a person fallen into the depths of misery or sin we must be kind to him, take him by the hand, help him to regain his footing, his strength; we must guide him with love and tenderness, treat him as a friend not as an enemy. We have no right to look upon any of our fellow-mortals as evil.

Concerning the prejudice of race: it is an illusion, a superstition pure and simple! For God created us all of one race. There were no differences in the beginning, for we are all descendants of Adam. In the beginning, also, there were no limits and boundaries between the different lands; no part of the earth belonged more to one people than to another. In the sight of God there is no difference between the various races. Why should man invent such a prejudice? How can we uphold war caused by an illusion?

God has not created men that they should destroy one another. All races, tribes, sects and classes share equally in the Bounty of their Heavenly Father.

The only difference lies in the degree of faithfulness, of obedience to the laws of God. There are some who are as lighted torches, there are others who shine as stars in the sky of humanity. The lovers of mankind, these are the superior men, of whatever nation, creed, or colour they may be. For it is they to whom God will say these blessed words, 'Well done, My good and faithful servants'. In that day He will not ask, 'Are you English, French, or perhaps Persian? Do you come from the East, or from the West?'

The only division that is real is this: There are heavenly men and earthly men; self-sacrificing servants of humanity in the love of the Most High, bringing harmony and unity, teaching peace and goodwill to men. On the other hand, there are those selfish men, haters of their brethren, in whose hearts prejudice has replaced loving kindness, and whose influence breeds discord and strife.

To which race or to which colour belong these two divisions of men, to the White, to the Yellow, to the Black, to the East or to the West, to the North or to the South? If these are God's divisions, why should we invent others? Political prejudice is equally mischievous, it is one of the greatest causes of bitter strife amongst the children of men. There are people who find pleasure in breeding discord, who constantly endeavour to goad their country into making war upon other nations—and why? They think to advantage their own country to the detriment of all others. They send armies to harass and destroy the land, in order to become famous in the world, for the joy of conquest. That it may be said: 'Such a country has defeated another, and brought it under the yoke of their stronger, more superior rule.' This victory, bought at the price of much bloodshed, is not lasting! The conqueror shall one day be conquered; and the vanquished ones victorious! Remember the history of the past: did not France conquer Germany more than once—then did not the German nation overcome France?

We learn also that France conquered England; then was the English nation victorious over France!

These glorious conquests are so ephemeral! Why attach so great importance to them and to their fame, as to be willing to shed the blood of the people for their attainment? Is any victory worth the inevitable train of evils consequent upon human slaughter, the grief and sorrow and ruin which must overwhelm so many homes of both nations? For it is not possible that one country alone should suffer.

Oh! why will man, the disobedient child of God, who should be an example of the power of the spiritual law, turn his face away from the Divine Teaching and put all his effort into destruction and war?

My hope is that in this enlightened century the Divine Light of love will shed its radiance over the whole world, seeking out the responsive heart's intelligence of every human being; that the light of the Sun of Truth will lead politicians to shake off all the claims of prejudice and superstition, and with freed minds to follow the Policy of God: for Divine Politics are mighty, man's politics are feeble! God has created all the world, and bestows His Divine Bounty upon every creature.

Are we not the servants of God? Shall we neglect to follow our Master's Example, and ignore His Commands?

I pray that the Kingdom shall come on Earth, and that all darkness shall be driven away by the effulgence of the Heavenly Sun.[32]

'Abdu'l-Bahá

9

Secular Government

The goal of many fundamentalists is to establish a government under the direction and control of clerics. This ensures the strict enforcement of the outward trappings of religion, but the real utility is that women, free expression, domestic criticism, and the exchange of competing ideas can be repressed. Truth can stand the fiercest of fires and the most relentless attacks, but those with questionable theology or ideology have difficulty allowing debate and free expression. Fanaticism takes choice out of religion, but this is a very hollow victory. Spirituality requires faith to be a matter of conscience, not compulsion.

> Faith of God must be propagated through human perfections, through qualities that are excellent and pleasing, and spiritual behavior. If a soul of his own accord advances toward God he will be accepted at the Threshold of Oneness, for such a one is free of personal considerations, of greed and selfish interests, and he has taken refuge within the sheltering protection of his Lord. He will become known among men as trustworthy and truthful, temperate and scrupulous, high-minded and loyal, incorruptible and God-fearing. In this way the primary purpose in revealing the Divine Law—which is to bring about happiness in the after life and civilization and the refinement of character in this—will be realized. As for the sword, it will only

produce a man who is outwardly a believer, and inwardly a traitor and apostate.

'Abdu'l-Bahá

It is undeniably beneficial for leaders in government to address the problems confronting mankind from a spiritual perspective. However, these leaders must also be well-acquainted with the needs and aspirations of the governed, moreover, they must be proficient in law, administration, and social sciences. This can best be achieved by a secular representative democracy. During another talk in Paris, 'Abdu'l-Bahá explained:

> If administrators of the law would take into consideration the spiritual consequences of their decisions, and follow the guidance of religion, 'They would be Divine agents in the world of action, the representatives of God for those who are on earth, and they would defend, for the love of God, the interests of His servants as they would defend their own.' If a governor realizes his responsibility, and fears to defy the Divine Law, his judgements will be just. Above all, if he believes that the consequences of his actions will follow him beyond his earthly life, and that 'as he sows so must he reap', such a man will surely avoid injustice and tyranny.
>
> Should an official, on the contrary, think that all responsibility for his actions must end with his earthly life, knowing and believing nothing of Divine favours and a spiritual kingdom of joy, he will lack the incentive to just dealing, and the inspiration to destroy oppression and unrighteousness.
>
> When a ruler knows that his judgements will be weighed in a balance by the Divine Judge, and that if he be not found wanting he will come into the Celestial Kingdom and that the light of the Heavenly Bounty will shine upon

him, then will he surely act with justice and equity. Behold how important it is that Ministers of State should be enlightened by religion!

With political questions the clergy, however, have nothing to do! Religious matters should not be confused with politics in the present state of the world (for their interests are not identical). Religion concerns matters of the heart, of the spirit, and of morals.

Politics are occupied with the material things of life. Religious teachers should not invade the realm of politics; they should concern themselves with the spiritual education of the people; they should ever give good counsel to men, trying to serve God and human kind; they should endeavour to awaken spiritual aspiration, and strive to enlarge the understanding and knowledge of humanity, to improve morals, and to increase the love for justice.

This is in accordance with the Teaching of Bahá'u'lláh. In the Gospel also it is written, 'Render unto Caesar the things which are Caesar's, and unto God the things which are God's...'

Oh, friends of God, be living examples of justice! So that by the Mercy of God, the world may see in your actions that you manifest the attributes of justice and mercy.

Justice is not limited, it is a universal quality. Its operation must be carried out in all classes, from the highest to the lowest. Justice must be sacred, and the rights of all the people must be considered. Desire for others only that which you desire for yourselves. Then shall we rejoice in the Sun of Justice, which shines from the Horizon of God.

Each man has been placed in a post of honour, which he must not desert. A humble workman who commits an injustice is as much to blame as a renowned tyrant. Thus we all have our choice between justice and injustice.

I hope that each one of you will become just, and direct
your thoughts towards the unity of mankind; that you will
never harm your neighbours nor speak ill of any one; that
you will respect the rights of all men, and be more
concerned for the interests of others than for your own.
Thus will you become torches of Divine justice, acting in
accordance with the Teaching of Bahá'u'lláh, who, during
His life, bore innumerable trials and persecutions in order
to show forth to the world of mankind the virtues of the
World of Divinity, making it possible for you to realize the
supremacy of the spirit, and to rejoice in the Justice of
God.[33]

                                              'Abdu'l-Bahá

10
Theocracy

In the West, theocracy is primarily associated with fundamentalist Islamic states. Let us not forget, however, that a thousand years ago, Northern Europe was in the midst of the Dark Ages and the titular head of the Christian church wielded enormous political power. The Vatican actively suppressed scientific research and its dissemination, and punished those whose ideas challenged church dogma. During this time Islam produced an enlightened culture, known for tolerance, knowledge, scholarship and progress. Muslim scholars were at the forefront in philosophy, medicine, and mathematics. Universities in Islamic cities were academic hubs with thousands of books at a time in which Europe was steeped in ignorance and superstition. Cordoba, capital city of Islamic Spain, was the pinnacle of culture in Europe. Its library contained 400,000 volumes at a time when the largest library in Christian Europe, St. Gall in Switzerland, possessed only a few hundred books.

Let us recall that it was the head of the Christian church, Pope Urban II, who called for the faithful to wage a holy war. Those who took part were promised honour, paradise and the forgiveness of sins. Bloodthirsty crusaders could not wait to encounter the enemy, so they pillaged, extorted and murdered fellow Christians on their way to fight the "infidels". Once Jerusalem was taken, the crusaders burned three hundred Jews alive in a synagogue, and murdered every Muslim woman and child they found on the Temple Mount. Unquestionably, the commingling of church and state brought out the worst of both institutions.

An oppressed and haggard peasant population in Europe was forced to support ruling classes of nobility and clergy. Women, especially the independent ones, were often in precarious circumstances and vulnerable to charges of witchcraft. The inquisition employed terror and torture to achieve orthodoxy and theological purity. It was forbidden to translate the *Bible* into the vernacular of the people, thus believers knew only what the clergy wanted them to know.

Not until the sixteenth century did lay people have access to a translation of the *Bible*, when it was translated into German by Martin Luther. Not only were other religions persecuted, but a series of horrific wars, some lasting decades, were fought between Catholics and emerging Christian reform movements. Religious affiliation was generally not a question of conscience, rather it was a matter of adopting the religion of one's feudal master. Even today in Germany, religious affiliation is a product of those bygone theocratic power struggles. Thus the various states in Germany tend to be either predominately Catholic or Lutheran and even today do not share identical religious holidays.

During the conquests of the two American continents indigenous people were sometimes faced with the choice of death or forced conversion. Indeed, in the not too distant past, native North Americans were prevented from practising their religion, and their children were forced to attend boarding schools where they were raised as Christians. So the secular, tolerant Christian state was a long time in coming.

Actually it was a bit of a twist of fate that the persecution of Protestant movements in Europe played a part in the development of the secular state in America. The New World was in part settled by Protestant groups seeking religious freedom, and the resulting diversity of belief was partly responsible for the United States being founded as a nation under God, but with a clear separation between church and state. The question of church and state led President Thomas Jefferson, the author of America's Declaration of Independence, to observe: "United we stand, Divided we fall."

When we in the West consider the centuries it took to separate church and state, we should have a degree of humility and understanding when we consider the desire of fundamentalist Muslims to create theocratic societies. They tend to see theocratic government as the solution to their problems. The problem, in their view, is modernity, liberty, free expression, personal choice, competing ideas, and temptation (which they believe can be overcome with force). Writing in 1990, Professor Bernard Lewis wrote a piece which analysed Muslim rage. He identified several root causes, one of which was a movement among Muslim intellectuals, many of whom had studied in Europe in the mid-twentieth century. Angered by the legacy of European colonialism, they rejected Western civilisation and portrayed America, the Western superpower, as the primary enemy. According to the motto, he who is the enemy of my enemy is my friend, they often looked to anti-American fascists governments and East Bloc totalitarian regimes for support and inspiration. Perhaps this helps to explain in part why several Islamic nations have one party governments, no free press, brutal secret police, and strongman dictators with their portraits plastered on public buildings. One can make the case that a number of the problems associated with Middle Eastern authoritarian states can be traced back to the rejection of Western democratic ideals by these radicalised student intellectuals and fanatical clerics. Of course, the foreign policy expediency associated with expanding and maintaining of the Soviet and American spheres of influence during the cold war, also played a role, as does the economic necessity of maintaining access to Middle Eastern oil.

In 1875, 'Abdu'l-Bahá authored a book addressed to the Muslims of Persia which dealt with the development of civilisation, and questioned the wisdom of rejecting ideas which originate from Christians:

> As to those who maintain that the inauguration of reforms and the setting up of powerful institutions would in reality be at variance with the good pleasure of God and would contravene the laws of the Divine Law-Giver and run counter to basic religious principles and to the ways of the Prophet—let them consider how this could be the case. Would such reforms contravene the religious law because they would be acquired from foreigners and would therefore cause us to be as they are, since "He who imitates a people is one of them"? In the first place these matters relate to the temporal and material apparatus of civilization, the implements of science, the adjuncts of progress in the professions and the arts, and the orderly conduct of government. They have nothing whatever to do with the problems of the spirit and the complex realities of religious doctrine. If it be objected that even where material affairs are concerned foreign importations are inadmissible, such an argument would only establish the ignorance and absurdity of its proponents. Have they forgotten the celebrated hádith (Holy Tradition): "Seek after knowledge, even unto China"? [34]

'Abdu'l-Bahá

In the mid-nineteenth century, Bahá'u'lláh revealed an epistle to Queen Victoria in which He not only affirmed representative democracy, but counselled the representatives to look beyond their own immediate concerns and address themselves to the betterment of the world:

We have also heard that thou hast entrusted the reins of counsel into the hands of the representatives of the people. Thou, indeed, hast done well, for thereby the foundations of the edifice of thine affairs will be strengthened, and the hearts of all that are beneath thy shadow, whether high or low, will be tranquillized. It behoveth them, however, to be trustworthy among His servants, and to regard themselves as the representatives of all that dwell on earth.[35]

Bahá'u'lláh

Personally, for me to imagine a workable theocracy, several prerequisites, lacking in Judaism, Christianity, and Islam, would be necessary. First, mankind would need to be united in faith. It could not be an imposed faith, but would need to be a genuine faith of conscience. Secondly, the framework of such a theocratic government would need to be contained in the scriptures accepted by all. An acceptable theocratic government would have to be democratically elected to a specific term, and representation could not be limited to clerics or clergy. At the same time, to maintain its spiritual underpinnings it would need to avoid the divisiveness of bitter partisan politics. Its theocratic framework, based upon unambiguous scripture, would need to establish a clear and recognised body which could enact laws dealing with situations not found in the scriptures. Since circumstances change, representatives would need to be able to amend or repeal laws enacted by their predecessors. Such a government would need to be dedicated to establishing justice and fairness in all facets of human existence. Finally, it would need to respect cultural diversity and unswervingly follow the path of moderation.

11
Monotheism

Since the populations of Europe and the American continents are predominately Christian, they tend to think of Christianity as a Western religion. While it is known, it is somehow not truly acknowledged that Jesus was a Jew born in Bethlehem in Judea. His mother, brothers, and sisters were all Jews, as were His apostles and early followers. Jesus made clear that He did not come to abrogate Judaism, rather He came to renew, expand, and fulfil it.

Since one was primarily born into Judaism, monotheism, in a certain sense, was a tribal religion prior to Jesus. Peter, one of Jesus' original disciples, saw his mission as bringing the message of Jesus to his fellow Jews. Paul, however, a Jew born as Saul in Tarsus in what is now Turkey, saw his mission as taking the message of Christ to the gentiles (non-Jews). Initially the early followers of Jesus were quite Jewish in their adherence to circumcision, dietary restrictions, and other aspects of Jewish law. Peter did eventually support Paul's opinion that converts to Christianity need not be circumcised nor follow biblical dietary restrictions. Thus Paul played an instrumental role in bringing the monotheism of Judaism to the gentiles in Europe. With the expansion of monotheism beyond the tribes of Israel, the belief in the One God became a matter of conscience not conditioned upon birth.

Christianity changed Europe, but European thought also changed the monotheism of Judaism which Jesus taught. The dogma of the Trinity, developed from the second through the fourth centuries, demanded that Christ been seen as God in the flesh, the incarnate Son of God, God from God. It became heresy to consider Him a mighty Prophet conceived immaculately of a virgin, imbued with the Spirit of God, and charged with a mission to reveal God's guidance to mankind.

Not all Christians agreed with the Trinity, but orthodoxy prevailed over conscience. Monarchianism was a movement in the second and third centuries which sought to restore monotheism to Christianity, but its adherents were persecuted as heretics. Similarly, Nestorianism spread quickly in Eastern Orthodox areas in the fifth century, but its followers were also persecuted and forced to flee to Persia, India and even China. Finally, the Unitarian movement can be traced back to the sixteenth century, when in 1553 a Spanish physician, Michael Servtus, was burned at the stake for writing a book which questioned the Trinity.

Early Unitarians rejected the dogma of the Trinity, believing instead in the unity of God. Interestingly, the first edict for religious freedom in Europe was issued in 1568 by Europe's sole Unitarian ruler, King Sigismund of Transylvania. The movement spread into Poland and eventually into England in the seventeenth century. Today Unitarianism represents a liberal free thinking movement and the views of its membership are highly variegated. Most still see Jesus as a central figure in mankind's spiritual development, but His station might vary from that of an inspired prophet, to a wise teacher, or even a mythical figure.

In any case, unquestionably the shift away from the unambiguous monotheism of Judaism makes it difficult for Jews to embrace the teachings of the Christian churches. Indeed, one wonders if the concept of the Trinity would have become so dominant had more Jews accepted Jesus' teachings. 'Abdu'l-Bahá was asked to explain the concept of the Trinity, the three Gods in One, and gave this explanation:

> The Divine Reality, which is purified and sanctified from the understanding of human beings and which can never be imagined by the people of wisdom and of intelligence, is exempt from all conception. That Lordly Reality admits of no division; for division and multiplicity are properties of creatures which are contingent existences, and not accidents which happen to the self-existent.
>
> The Divine Reality is sanctified from singleness, then how much more from plurality. The descent of that Lordly Reality into conditions and degrees would be equivalent to imperfection and contrary to perfection, and is, therefore, absolutely impossible. It perpetually has been, and is, in the exaltation of holiness and sanctity. All that is mentioned of the Manifestations and Dawning places of God signifies the divine reflection, and not a descent into the conditions of existence.
>
> God is pure perfection, and creatures are but imperfections. For God to descend into the conditions of existence would be the greatest of imperfections; on the contrary, His manifestation, His appearance, His rising are like the reflection of the sun in a clear, pure, polished mirror. All the creatures are evident signs of God, like the earthly beings upon all of which the rays of the sun shine. But upon the plains, the mountains, the trees and fruits, only a portion of the light shines, through which they become visible, and are reared, and attain to the object of their existence, while the Perfect Man [The Divine Manifestation] is in the condition of a clear mirror in which the Sun of Reality becomes visible and manifest with all its qualities and perfections. So the Reality of Christ was a clear and polished mirror of the greatest purity and fineness. The Sun of Reality, the Essence of Divinity, reflected itself in this mirror

and manifested its light and heat in it; but from the exaltation of its holiness, and the heaven of its sanctity, the Sun did not descend to dwell and abide in the mirror. No, it continues to subsist in its exaltation and sublimity, while appearing and becoming manifest in the mirror in beauty and perfection.

Now if we say that we have seen the Sun in two mirrors—one the Christ and one the Holy Spirit—that is to say, that we have seen three Suns, one in heaven and the two others on the earth, we speak truly. And if we say that there is one Sun, and it is pure singleness, and has no partner and equal, we again speak truly.

The epitome of the discourse is that the Reality of Christ was a clear mirror, and the Sun of Reality—that is to say, the Essence of Oneness, with its infinite perfections and attributes—became visible in the mirror. The meaning is not that the Sun, which is the Essence of the Divinity, became divided and multiplied—for the Sun is one—but it appeared in the mirror. This is why Christ said, "The Father is in the Son," meaning that the Sun is visible and manifest in this mirror.

The Holy Spirit is the Bounty of God which becomes visible and evident in the Reality of Christ. The Sonship station is the heart of Christ, and the Holy Spirit is the station of the spirit of Christ. Hence it has become certain and proved that the Essence of Divinity is absolutely unique and has no equal, no likeness, no equivalent.

This is the signification of the Three Persons of the Trinity. If 'it were otherwise, the foundations of the Religion of God would rest upon an illogical proposition which the mind could never conceive, and how can the mind be forced to believe a thing which it cannot conceive? A thing cannot be grasped by the intelligence except when it is clothed in an intelligible form; otherwise, it is but an effort of the imagination.

It has now become clear, from this explanation, what is the meaning of the Three Persons of the Trinity. The Oneness of God is also proved.[36]

Integral to the Christian concept of the Trinity is that Jesus was the only Son of God. 'Abdu'l-Bahá was asked about this too and gave the following response:

Furthermore, in the first chapter of the Gospel of John, verses 12 and 13, it is said: "But as many as received Him, to them gave He power to become the sons of God, even to them that believed on His name:

"Which were born, not of blood, nor of the will of the flesh, nor of the will of man, but of God."

From these verses it is obvious that the being of a disciple also is not created by physical power, but by the spiritual reality. The honor and greatness of Christ is not due to the fact that He did not have a human father, but to His perfections, bounties and divine glory. If the greatness of Christ is His being fatherless, then Adam is greater than Christ, for He had neither father nor mother. It is said in the *Old Testament*, "And the Lord God formed man of the dust of the ground, and breathed into his nostrils the breath of life; and man became a living soul."[Gen. 2:7.] Observe that it is said that Adam came into existence from the Spirit of life. Moreover, the expression which John uses in regard to the disciples proves that they also are from the Heavenly Father. Hence it is evident that the holy reality, meaning the real existence of every great man, comes from God and owes its being to the breath of the Holy Spirit.

The purport is that, if to be without a father is the greatest human glory, then Adam is greater than all, for He had neither father nor mother. Is it better for a man to be created from a living substance or from earth? Certainly it is better if he be created from a living substance. But Christ was born and came into existence from the Holy Spirit.

To conclude: the splendor and honor of the holy souls and the Divine Manifestations come from Their heavenly perfections, bounties and glory, and from nothing else.[37]

As someone who was raised as a Christian to love and revere Jesus Christ, it puzzles me why the early European Christians felt the need to shift the emphasis away from His Sermon on the Mount, and to stress instead His birth and death. He certainly did not focus on this aspect of His being, He was much more interested in spreading His message of love and spirituality. Moreover, he maintained that His message, like that of the Prophets before Him, was from God:

My doctrine is not mine, but His that sent me.[38]

Jesus

But now ye seek to kill me,
a man that hath told you the truth,
which I have heard of God:
this did not Abraham? [39]

Jesus

Even today one hears some members of the Christian clergy who unabashedly proclaim to an international television audience that only those who share their interpretation of the *New Testament* will avoid damnation. By contrast, Muhammad was extraordinarily tolerant with respect to Judaism and Christianity. His was a mission to rescue the world from polytheism and idolatry. Christians and Jews were welcomed to become Muslims, but only when the decision was completely voluntary. Muhammad was perfectly willing to live alongside

Jews and Christians and to protect them from outside threats. However, He rejected their claims that salvation was reserved for followers of a particular religion. He maintained that whosoever believes in God and does good deeds, has nothing to fear. He encouraged Jews, Christians and Muslims to vie with one another in doing good works. He taught that in the end all will return to God and be informed of how they differ.

While He did not require Jews and Christians to accept Him as a Prophet, He did require those who became Muslims to acknowledge the prophethood of Abraham, Ishmael, Isaac, Jacob, Moses and Jesus. He acknowledged the virgin birth of Jesus and called Him the Spirit of God. He commanded Muslims not to make any distinction between the Prophets of God. He claimed nothing more for Himself than being a Messenger from God, the like of which had come before Him.

Thus He required Muslims to accept Jesus in order to be accepted before God, fulfilling the command that no one comes to the Father except through the Son. He did, however, point out to Christians the error of their claims about the station of Jesus as God. He proclaimed the Trinity was a misunderstanding by church leaders and insisted that Jesus taught His followers to worship only God, not Himself, nor His mother, whom Muhammad described as a saintly woman.

It is unfortunate that many Christians are unaware that Muhammad praised Jesus as the Spirit of God, a Prophet with special gifts from God. The fact that Muslims are reluctant to translate "Allah" from Arabic into other languages as "God" is also an unfortunate source of misunderstanding. One frequently hears comments that Jews and Christians worship the God of Jacob, but Muslims worship a man-made god they call Allah.

Monotheism should be the glue which joins Jews, Christians, and Muslims together. To see the children of the same God harbouring ill-will, resentment, and enmity towards one another is an anathema to the Creator they claim to love and obey. To kill one another in His name is blasphemy. If asked to imagine the most horrific event for a parent, you would probably answer with the death of a child. But imagine a parent's pain if one child kills its sibling. Then imagine the child believing he did it in the name of the parent. At this moment in time, the inability of Christians, Muslims, and Jews to live in peace represents the greatest danger to the entire human race. It is necessary for ordinary believers of each religion, not just their prominent representatives, to reflect upon their own faith and examine their relationship to our common Creator. The children of God cannot continue to believe that He favours only one child, God is the Father of all.

> The earth is one native land, one home; and all mankind are the children of one Father. God has created them, and they are the recipients of His compassion. Therefore, if anyone offends another, he offends God. It is the wish of our heavenly Father that every heart should rejoice and be filled with happiness, that we should live together in felicity and joy. The obstacle to human happiness is racial or religious prejudice, the competitive struggle for existence and inhumanity toward each other.
>
> Your eyes have been illumined, your ears are attentive, your hearts knowing. You must be free from prejudice and fanaticism, beholding no differences between the races and religions. You must look to God, for He is the real Shepherd, and all humanity are His sheep. He loves them and loves them equally. As this is true, should the sheep quarrel among themselves? They should manifest gratitude and thankfulness to God, and the best way to thank God is to love one another.[40]
>
> *'Abdu'l-Bahá*

Each group continues to insists on the supremacy of the Prophet who founded its religion. The Prophets, however, were not concerned with personal glory, rather they dedicated themselves to educating mankind by spreading God's message. Alone and unaided, they raised the call and established religions which transformed the lives of millions of their followers over centuries of time. Their unity becomes apparent when we examine their lives, missions, and achievements in this light. Seeing this unity is an important step to overcoming emotional reactions which otherwise can lead to intolerance and fanaticism. In the following section the significance of Abraham, Moses, Jesus Christ, and Muhammad is summarised by 'Abdu'l-Bahá.

12

'Abdu'l-Bahá Speaks of Abraham

One of those Who possessed this power and was assisted by it was Abraham. And the proof of it was that He was born in Mesopotamia, and of a family who were ignorant of the Oneness of God. He opposed His own nation and people, and even His own family, by rejecting all their gods. Alone and without help He resisted a powerful tribe, a task which is neither simple nor easy. It is as if in this day someone were to go to a Christian people who are attached to the *Bible*, and deny Christ; or in the Papal Court—God forbid!—if such a one were in the most powerful manner to blaspheme against Christ and oppose the people.

These people believed not in one God but in many gods, to whom they ascribed miracles; therefore, they all arose against Him, and no one supported Him except Lot, His brother's son, and one or two other people of no importance. At last, reduced to the utmost distress by the opposition of His enemies, He was obliged to leave His native land. In reality they banished Him in order that He might be crushed and destroyed, and that no trace of Him might be left.

Abraham then came into the region of the Holy Land. His enemies considered that His exile would lead to His destruction and ruin, as it seemed impossible that a man banished from His native land, deprived of His rights and oppressed on all sides—

even though He were a king —could escape extermination. But Abraham stood fast and showed forth extraordinary firmness— and God made this exile to be to His eternal honor—until He established the Unity of God in the midst of a polytheistic generation. This exile became the cause of the progress of the descendants of Abraham, and the Holy Land was given to them. As a result the teachings of Abraham were spread abroad, a Jacob appeared among His posterity, and a Joseph who became ruler in Egypt. In consequence of His exile a Moses and a being like Christ were manifested from His posterity, and Hagar was found from whom Ishmael was born, one of whose descendants was Muhammad. In consequence of His exile the Báb appeared from His posterity [The Báb's descent was from Muhammad] and the Prophets of Israel were numbered among the descendants of Abraham. And so it will continue for ever and ever. Finally, in consequence of His exile the whole of Europe and most of Asia came under the protecting shadow of the God of Israel. See what a power it is that enabled a Man Who was a fugitive from His country to found such a family, to establish such a faith, and to promulgate such teachings. Can anyone say that all this occurred accidentally? We must be just: was this Man an Educator or not?

Since the exile of Abraham from Ur to Aleppo in Syria produced this result, we must consider what will be the effect of the exile of Bahá'u'lláh in His several removes from Tihran to Baghdad, from thence to Constantinople, to Rumelia and to the Holy Land.

See what a perfect Educator Abraham was!

'Abdu'l-Bahá

13
'Abdu'l-Bahá Speaks of Moses

At a time when the Israelites had multiplied in Egypt and were spread throughout the whole country, the Coptic Pharaohs of Egypt determined to strengthen and favor their own Coptic peoples and to degrade and dishonor the children of Israel, whom they regarded as foreigners. Over a long period, the Israelites, divided and scattered, were captive in the hands of the tyrannical Copts, and were scorned and despised by all, so that the meanest of the Copts would freely persecute and lord it over the noblest of the Israelites. The enslavement, wretchedness and helplessness of the Hebrews reached such a pitch that they were never, day or night, secure in their own persons nor able to provide any defense for their wives and families against the tyranny of their Pharaohic captors. Then their food was the fragments of their own broken hearts, and their drink a river of tears. They continued on in this anguish until suddenly Moses, the All-Beauteous, beheld the Divine Light streaming out of the blessed Vale, the place that was holy ground, and heard the quickening voice of God as it spoke from the flame of that Tree "neither of the East nor of the West,"[41] and He stood up in the full panoply of His universal prophethood. In the midst of the Israelites, He blazed out like a lamp of Divine guidance, and by the light of salvation He led that lost people out of the shadows of ignorance into knowledge and perfection. He gathered Israel's scattered tribes into the shelter of the unifying and universal Word of God, and over the heights of union He raised up the banner of harmony, so that within a brief interval those benighted souls became spiritually educated, and they who had been strangers to the truth, rallied to the cause of the oneness of God, and were delivered out of their wretchedness, their indigence, their incomprehension and captivity and achieved a supreme degree of happiness and honor. They emigrated from Egypt, set out for Israel's original homeland, and came to Canaan and Philistia. They first conquered the shores of the River Jordan, and Jericho, and settled in that area, and ultimately all the neighboring regions, such as Phoenicia, Edom and Ammon, came under their sway. In Joshua's time there were thirty-one governments in the hands of the Israelites, and in every noble human attribute—learning, stability, determination, courage, honor, generosity—this people came to surpass all the nations of the earth. When in those days an Israelite would enter a gathering, he was immediately singled out for his many virtues, and even foreign peoples wishing to praise a man would say that he was like an Israelite.

It is furthermore a matter of record in numerous historical works that the philosophers of Greece such as Pythagoras, acquired the major part of their philosophy, both divine and material, from the disciples of Solomon. And Socrates after having eagerly journeyed to meet with some of Israel's most illustrious scholars and divines, on his return to Greece established the concept of the oneness of God and the continuing life of the human soul after it has put off its elemental dust. Ultimately, the ignorant among the Greeks denounced this man who had fathomed the inmost mysteries of wisdom, and rose up to take his life; and then the populace forced the hand of their ruler, and in council assembled they caused Socrates to drink from the poisoned cup.

After the Israelites had advanced along every level of civilization, and had achieved success in the highest possible degree, they began little by little to forget the root-principles of the Mosaic Law and Faith, to busy themselves with rites and ceremonials and to show forth unbecoming conduct. In the days of Rehoboam, the son of Solomon, terrible dissension broke out among them; one of their number, Jeroboam, plotted to get the throne, and it was he who introduced the worship of idols. The strife between Rehoboam and Jeroboam led to centuries of warfare between their descendants, with the result that the tribes of Israel were scattered and disrupted. In brief, it was because they forgot the meaning of the Law of God that they became involved in ignorant fanaticism and blameworthy practices such as insurgence and sedition. Their divines, having concluded that all those essential qualifications of humankind set forth in the Holy Book were by then a dead letter, began to think only of furthering their own selfish interests, and afflicted the people by allowing them to sink into the lowest depths of heedlessness and ignorance. And the fruit of their wrong doing was this, that the old-time glory which had endured so long now changed to degradation, and the rulers of Persia, of Greece, and of Rome, took them over.

The banners of their sovereignty were reversed; the ignorance, foolishness, abasement and self-love of their religious leaders and their scholars were brought to light in the coming of Nebuchadnezzar, King of Babylon, who destroyed them. After a general massacre, and the sacking and razing of their houses and even the uprooting of their trees, he took captive whatever remnants his sword had spared and carried them off to Babylon. Seventy years later the descendants of these captives were released and went back to Jerusalem. Then Hezekiah and Ezra re-established in their midst the fundamental principles of the Holy Book, and day by day the Israelites advanced, and the morning-brightness of their earlier ages dawned again. In a short time, however, great dissensions as to belief and conduct broke out anew, and again the one concern of the Jewish doctors became the promotion of their own selfish purposes, and the reforms that had obtained in Ezra's time were changed to perversity and corruption. The situation worsened to such a degree that time and again, the armies of the republic of Rome and of its rulers conquered Israelite territory. Finally, the warlike Titus, commander of the Roman forces, trampled the Jewish homeland into dust, putting every man to the sword, taking the women and children captive, flattening their houses, tearing out their trees, burning their books, looting their treasures, and reducing Jerusalem and the Temple to an ash heap. After this supreme calamity, the star of Israel's dominion sank away to nothing, and to this day, the remnant of that vanished nation has been scattered to the four winds. [42]

'Abdu'l-Bahá

14

Abdu'l-Bahá Speaks of Jesus Christ

When for the second time the unmistakable signs of Israel's disintegration, abasement, subjection and annihilation had become apparent, then the sweet and holy breathings of the Spirit of God (Jesus) were shed across Jordan and the land of Galilee; the cloud of Divine pity overspread those skies, and rained down the copious waters of the spirit, and after those swelling showers that came from the most great Sea, the Holy Land put forth its perfume and blossomed with the knowledge of God. Then the solemn Gospel song rose up till it rang in the ears of those who dwell in the chambers of heaven, and at the touch of Jesus' breath the unmindful dead that lay in the graves of their ignorance lifted up their heads to receive eternal life. For the space of three years, that Luminary of perfections walked about the fields of Palestine and in the neighborhood of Jerusalem, leading all men into the dawn of redemption, teaching them how to acquire spiritual qualities and attributes well-pleasing to God. Had the people of Israel believed in that beauteous Countenance, they would have girded themselves to serve and obey Him heart and soul, and through the quickening fragrance of His Spirit they would have regained their lost vitality and gone on to new victories.

Alas, of what avail was it; they turned away and opposed Him. They rose up and tormented that Source of Divine

knowledge, that Point where the Revelation had come down—
all except for a handful who, turning their faces toward God,
were cleansed of the stain of this world and found their way to
the heights of the placeless Realm. They inflicted every agony
on that Wellspring of grace until it became impossible for Him
to live in the towns, and still He lifted up the flag of salvation
and solidly established the fundamentals of human righteousness,
that essential basis of true civilization.

In the fifth chapter of *Matthew* beginning with the thirty-
seventh verse He counsels: "Resist not evil and injury with its
like; but whosoever shall smite thee on thy right cheek, turn to
him the other also." And further, from the forty-third verse: "Ye
have heard that it hath been said, 'Thou shalt love thy neighbor,
and thou shalt not vex thine enemy with enmity.' [43] But I say
unto you, love your enemies, bless them that curse you, do good
to them that hate you, and pray for them which despitefully use
you, and persecute you; that ye may be the children of your
Father which is in heaven: for He maketh His sun to rise on the
evil and on the good, and sendeth down the rain of His mercy
on the just and on the unjust. For if ye love them which love
you, what reward have ye? Do not even the publicans the same?"

Many were the counsels of this kind that were uttered by
that Dayspring of Divine wisdom, and souls who have become
characterized with such attributes of holiness are the distilled
essence of creation and the sources of true civilization.

Jesus, then, founded the sacred Law on a basis of moral
character and complete spirituality, and for those who believed
in Him He delineated a special way of life which constitutes the
highest type of action on earth. And while those emblems of
redemption were to outward seeming abandoned to the
malevolence and persecution of their tormentors, in reality they
had been delivered out of the hopeless darkness which
encompassed the Jews and they shone forth in everlasting glory
at the dawn of that new day.

That mighty Jewish nation toppled and crumbled away, but those few souls who sought shelter beneath the Messianic Tree transformed all human life. At that time the peoples of the world were utterly ignorant, fanatical and idolatrous. Only a small group of Jews professed belief in the oneness of God and they were wretched outcasts. These holy Christian souls now stood up to promulgate a Cause which was diametrically opposed and repugnant to the beliefs of the entire human race. The kings of four out of the world's five continents inexorably resolved to wipe out the followers of Christ, and nevertheless in the end most of them set about promoting the Faith of God with their whole hearts; all the nations of Europe, many of the peoples of Asia and Africa, and some of the inhabitants of the islands of the Pacific, were gathered into the shelter of the oneness of God.

Consider whether there exists anywhere in creation a principle mightier in every sense than religion, or whether any conceivable power is more pervasive than the various Divine Faiths, or whether any agency can bring about real love and fellowship and union among all peoples as can belief in an almighty and all-knowing God, or whether except for the laws of God there has been any evidence of an instrumentality for educating all mankind in every phase of righteousness.

Those qualities which the philosophers attained when they had reached the very heights of their wisdom, those noble human attributes which characterized them at the peak of their perfection, would be exemplified by the believers as soon as they accepted the Faith. Observe how those souls who drank the living waters of redemption at the gracious hands of Jesus, the Spirit of God, and came into the sheltering shade of the *Gospel*, attained to such a high plane of moral conduct that Galen, the celebrated physician, although not himself a Christian, in his summary of Plato's *Republic* extolled their actions. A literal translation of his words is as follows:

"The generality of mankind are unable to grasp a sequence of logical arguments. For this reason they stand in need of symbols and parables telling of rewards and punishments in the next world. A confirmatory evidence of this is that today we observe a people called Christians, who believe devoutly in rewards and punishments in a future state. This group show forth excellent actions, similar to the actions of an individual who is a true philosopher. For example, we all see with our own eyes that they have no fear of death, and their passion for justice and fair-dealing is so great that they should be considered true philosophers."[44]

The station of a philosopher, in that age and in the mind of Galen, was superior to any other station in the world. Consider then how the enlightening and spiritualizing power of divine religions impels the believers to such heights of perfection that a philosopher like Galen, not himself a Christian, offers such testimony.

One demonstration of the excellent character of the Christians in those days was their dedication to charity and good works, and the fact that they founded hospitals and philanthropic institutions. For example, the first person to establish public clinics throughout the Roman Empire where the poor, the injured and the helpless received medical care, was the Emperor Constantine. This great king was the first Roman ruler to champion the Cause of Christ. He spared no efforts, dedicating his life to the promotion of the principles of the Gospel, and he solidly established the Roman government, which in reality had been nothing but a system of unrelieved oppression, on moderation and justice. His blessed name shines out across the dawn of history like the morning star, and his rank and fame among the world's noblest and most highly civilized is still on the tongues of Christians of all denominations.

What a firm foundation of excellent character was laid down in those days, thanks to the training of holy souls who arose to promote the teachings of the Gospel. How many primary schools, colleges, hospitals, were established, and institutions where fatherless and indigent children received their education. How many were the individuals who sacrificed their own personal advantages and "out of desire to please the Lord"[45] devoted the days of their lives to teaching the masses.

When, however, the time approached for the effulgent beauty of Muhammad to dawn upon the world, the control of Christian affairs passed into the hands of ignorant priests. Those heavenly breezes, soft-flowing from the regions of Divine grace, died away, and the laws of the great Evangel, the rock-foundation on which the civilization of the world was based, turned barren of results, this out of misuse and because of the conduct of persons who, seemingly fair, were yet inwardly foul.

The noted historians of Europe, in describing the conditions, manners, politics, learning and culture, in all their aspects, of early, medieval and modern times, unanimously record that during the ten centuries constituting the Middle Ages, from the beginning of the sixth century of the Christian era till the close of the fifteenth, Europe was in every respect and to an extreme degree, barbaric and dark. The principal cause of this was that the monks, referred to by European peoples as spiritual and religious leaders, had given up the abiding glory that comes from obedience to the sacred commandments and heavenly teachings of the Gospel, and had joined forces with the presumptuous and tyrannical rulers of the temporal governments of those times. They had turned their eyes away from everlasting glory, and were devoting all their efforts to the furtherance of their mutual worldly interests and passing and perishable advantages. Ultimately things reached a point where the masses were hopeless prisoners in the hands of these two groups, and all this brought down in ruins the whole structure of the religion, culture, welfare and civilisation of the peoples of Europe.[46]

'Abdu'l-Bahá

15
'Abdu'l-Bahá Speaks of Muhammad

Now we come to Muhammad. Americans and Europeans have heard a number of stories about the Prophet which they have thought to be true, although the narrators were either ignorant or antagonistic: most of them were clergy; others were ignorant Muslims who repeated unfounded traditions about Muhammad which they ignorantly believed to be to His praise.

Thus some benighted Muslims made His polygamy the pivot of their praises and held it to be a wonder, regarding it as a miracle; and European historians, for the most part, rely on the tales of these ignorant people.

For example, a foolish man said to a clergyman that the true proof of greatness is bravery and the shedding of blood, and that in one day on the field of battle a follower of Muhammad had cut off the heads of one hundred men! This misled the clergyman to infer that killing is considered the way to prove one's faith to Muhammad, while this is merely imaginary. The military expeditions of Muhammad, on the contrary, were always defensive actions: a proof of this is that during thirteen years, in Mecca, He and His followers endured the most violent persecutions. At this period they were the target for the arrows of hatred: some of His companions were killed and their property confiscated; others fled to foreign lands. Muhammad Himself, after the most extreme persecutions by the Qurayshites, who finally resolved to kill Him, fled to Medina in the middle of the night. Yet even then His enemies did not cease their persecutions, but pursued Him to Medina, and His disciples even to Abyssinia.

These Arab tribes were in the lowest depths of savagery and barbarism, and in comparison with them the savages of Africa and wild Indians of America were as advanced as a Plato. The savages of America do not bury their children alive as these Arabs did their daughters, glorying in it as being an honorable thing to do.[The Banu-Tamim, one of the most barbarous Arab tribes, practiced this odious custom.] Thus many of the men would threaten their wives, saying, "If a daughter is born to you, I will kill you." Even down to the present time the Arabs dread having daughters. Further, a man was permitted to take a thousand women, and most husbands had more than ten wives in their household. When these tribes made war, the one which was victorious would take the women and children of the vanquished tribe captive and treat them as slaves.

When a man who had ten wives died, the sons of these women rushed at each other's mothers; and if one of the sons threw his mantle over the head of his father's wife and cried out, "This woman is my lawful property," at once the unfortunate woman became his prisoner and slave. He could do whatever he wished with her. He could kill her, imprison her in a well, or beat, curse and torture her until death released her. According to the Arab habits and customs, he was her master. It is evident that malignity, jealousy, hatred and enmity must have existed between the wives and children of a household, and it is, therefore, needless to enlarge upon the subject. Again, consider what was the condition and life of these oppressed women! Moreover, the means by which these Arab tribes lived consisted in pillage and robbery, so that they were perpetually engaged in fighting and war, killing one another, plundering and devastating each other's property, and capturing women and children, whom they would sell to strangers. How often it happened that the daughters and sons of a prince, who spent their day in comfort and luxury, found themselves, when night fell, reduced to shame, poverty and captivity. Yesterday they were princes, today they are captives; yesterday they were great ladies, today they are slaves.

Muhammad received the Divine Revelation among these tribes, and after enduring thirteen years of persecution from them, He fled [to Medina]. But this people did not cease to oppress; they united to exterminate Him and all His followers. It was under such circumstances that Muhammad was forced to take up arms. This is the truth: we are not bigoted and do not wish to defend Him, but we are just, and we say what is just. Look at it with justice. If Christ Himself had been placed in such circumstances among such tyrannical and barbarous tribes, and if for thirteen years He with His disciples had endured all these trials with patience, culminating in flight from His native land—if in spite of this these lawless tribes continued to pursue Him, to slaughter the men, to pillage their property, and to capture their women and children—what would have been Christ's conduct with regard to them? If this oppression had fallen only upon Himself, He would have forgiven them, and such an act of forgiveness would have been most praiseworthy; but if He had seen that these cruel and bloodthirsty murderers wished to kill, to pillage and to injure all these oppressed ones, and to take captive the women and children, it is certain that He would have protected them and would have resisted the tyrants. What objection, then, can be taken to Muhammad's action? Is it this, that He did not, with His followers, and their women and children, submit to these savage tribes? To free these tribes from their bloodthirstiness was the greatest kindness, and to coerce and restrain them was a true mercy. They were like a man holding in his hand a cup of poison, which, when about to drink, a friend breaks and thus saves him. If Christ had been placed in similar circumstances, it is certain that with a conquering power He would have delivered the men, women and children from the claws of these bloodthirsty wolves.

Muhammad never fought against the Christians; on the contrary, He treated them kindly and gave them perfect freedom. A community of Christian people lived at Najran and were under His care and protection. Muhammad said, "If anyone infringes their rights, I Myself will be his enemy, and in the presence of God I will bring a charge against him." In the edicts which He promulgated it is clearly stated that the lives, properties and honor of the Christians and Jews are under the protection of God; and that if a Muhammadan married a Christian woman, the husband must not prevent her from going to church, nor oblige her to veil herself; and that if she died, he must place her remains in the care of the Christian clergy. Should the Christians desire to build a church, Islam ought to help them. In case of war between Islam and her enemies, the Christians should be exempted from the obligation of fighting, unless they desired of their own free will to do so in defense of Islam, because they were under its protection. But as a compensation for this immunity, they should pay yearly a small sum of money. In short, there are seven detailed edicts on these subjects, some copies of which are still extant at Jerusalem. This is an established fact and is not dependent on my affirmation. The edict of the second Caliph[Of Umar.] still exists in the custody of the orthodox Patriarch of Jerusalem, and of this there is no doubt.[47]

Nevertheless, after a certain time, and through the transgression of both the Muhammadans and the Christians, hatred and enmity arose between them. Beyond this fact, all the narrations of the Muslims, Christians and others are simply fabrications, which have their origin in fanaticism, or ignorance, or emanate from intense hostility.

For example, the Muslims say that Muhammad cleft the moon, and that it fell on the mountain of Mecca: they think that the moon is a small body which Muhammad divided into two parts and threw one part on this mountain, and the other part on another mountain.

Such stories are pure fanaticism. Also the traditions which the clergy quote, and the incidents with which they find fault, are all exaggerated, if not entirely without foundation.

Briefly, Muhammad appeared in the desert of Hijaz in the Arabian Peninsula, which was a desolate, sterile wilderness, sandy and uninhabited. Some parts, like Mecca and Medina, are extremely hot; the people are nomads with the manners and customs of the dwellers in the desert, and are entirely destitute of education and science. Muhammad Himself was illiterate, and the *Qur'an* was originally written upon the bladebones of sheep, or on palm leaves. These details indicate the condition of the people to whom Muhammad was sent. The first question which He put to them was, "Why do you not accept the *Pentateuch* and the *Gospel*, and why do you not believe in Christ and in Moses?" This saying presented difficulties to them, and they argued, "Our forefathers did not believe in the *Pentateuch* and the *Gospel*; tell us, why was this?" He answered, "They were misled; you ought to reject those who do not believe in the *Pentateuch* and the *Gospel*, even though they are your fathers and your ancestors."

In such a country, and amidst such barbarous tribes, an illiterate Man produced a book in which, in a perfect and eloquent style, He explained the divine attributes and perfections, the prophethood of the Messengers of God, the divine laws, and some scientific facts.

Thus, you know that before the observations of modern times—that is to say, during the first centuries and down to the fifteenth century of the Christian era—all the mathematicians of the world agreed that the earth was the center of the universe, and that the sun moved. The famous astronomer who was the protagonist of the new theory discovered the movement of the earth and the immobility of the sun [Copernicus]. Until his time all the astronomers and philosophers of the world followed the Ptolemaic system, and whoever said anything against it was considered ignorant. Though Pythagoras, and Plato during the latter part of his life, adopted the theory that the annual movement of the sun around the zodiac does not proceed from the sun, but rather from the movement of the earth around the sun, this theory had been entirely forgotten, and the Ptolemaic system was accepted by all mathematicians. But there are some verses revealed in the *Qur'an* contrary to the theory of the Ptolemaic system. One of them is "The sun moves in a fixed place," which shows the fixity of the sun, and its movement around an axis.[48] Again, in another verse, "And each star moves in its own heaven."[49] Thus is explained the movement of the sun, of the moon, of the earth, and of other bodies. When the *Qur'an* appeared, all the mathematicians ridiculed these statements and attributed the theory to ignorance. Even the doctors of Islam, when they saw that these verses were contrary to the accepted Ptolemaic system, were obliged to explain them away.

It was not until after the fifteenth century of the Christian era, nearly nine hundred years after Muhammad, that a famous astronomer made new observations and important discoveries by the aid of the telescope, which he had invented.[50] The rotation of the earth, the fixity of the sun, and also its movement around an axis, were discovered. It became evident that the verses of the *Qur'an* agreed with existing facts, and that the Ptolemaic system was imaginary.

In short, many Oriental peoples have been reared for thirteen centuries under the shadow of the religion of Muhammad. During the Middle Ages, while Europe was in the lowest depths of barbarism, the Arab peoples were superior to the other nations of the earth in learning, in the arts, mathematics, civilisation, government and other sciences. The Enlightener and Educator of these Arab tribes, and the Founder of the civilization and perfections of humanity among these different races, was an illiterate Man, Muhammad. Was this illustrious Man a thorough Educator or not? A just judgment is necessary.[51]

16
Judaism

Christians and Muslims should never overlook that Jews kept the flame of belief in the One True God alive over millennia, regardless of the tribulations and hardships which befell them. From their midst emerged a string of Prophets, beginning with Abraham and culminating in Jesus. This people can never be considered your enemy, they are your brothers in faith.

Throughout their early history it was essential for Jews to stand apart from others, while remaining together as a people. Their covenant was to keep belief in the One True God alive. Their strict observance of laws, customs, traditions, celebrations, and intermarriage kept them from losing their identity and ensured that belief in God would not be weakened. Steadfastly they kept their covenant with God. Jews can be proud of this tremendous achievement, but they need not stand apart any longer.

Jewish thought recognises the concept of theodicy (God's justice) and it holds that Jewish well-being and good fortune are causally related to their obedience to God's law. Jesus claimed to fulfil Jewish law, therefore, if His claim is true, Jews might reflect if the well-being of the Jewish people, and the world in general, would have been improved if they had recognised and been obedient to the *Torah* and to the teachings of Jesus. The answer to that question is in their heart of hearts.

I would ask Jews to look beyond the theology of the Christian church and concentrate on the teachings of Jesus. Perhaps, it would help to ignore the Greek translation of His Hebrew name and think of Him as Joshua, or Yehoshuah (Jehovah is deliverance). Ask yourselves, what harm can come to the Jewish people from recognising that Jesus was a mighty Jewish Prophet? He and His disciples spread the belief in the God of Jacob to every corner of the world. Christian dogma makes it difficult for Jews to see Jesus as He saw Himself, but the words in the *New Testament* attributed to Him will ring true.

Although Roman armies destroyed Jerusalem in A.D. 70, the emperors of the Roman Empire eventually ceased to be worshipped as gods and in due time they prayed to your God, the God of Jacob. Recognise what an incredible achievement that was, and what an honour it is that the most influential teacher in the history of mankind was a Jew. It is not necessary to stop thinking of yourselves as Jews in order to accept Jesus as a Prophet. Moreover, your understanding of the *Torah* could help Christians to better understand Jesus' teachings, and to return them to the unambiguous monotheism He taught.

On November 8, 1912, 'Abdu'l-Bahá spoke to a synagogue in Washington, D.C. This was, of course, several decades before the Holocaust. 'Abdu'l-Bahá spoke out of love, not with an eye to political correctness. He was concerned with the safety of the Jewish people if they continued to steadfastly reject Jesus' teachings as the word of God. He spoke very openly and frankly to the congregation, and the Rabbi visited him the next day to inform him that his talk had disturbed some of those present. 'Abdu'l-Bahá related their conversation which included this warning:

> The time may come when in Europe itself they will arise against the Jews. But your declaration that Christ was the Word of God will end all such trouble. My advice is that

in order to become honorable, protected and secure among the nations of the world, in order that the Christians may love and safeguard the Israelitish people, you should be willing to announce your belief in Christ, the Word of God.[52]

Here is a talk he delivered a month earlier at the Temple Emmanu-El in San Francisco, California:

The greatest bestowal of God in the world of humanity is religion, for assuredly the divine teachings of religion are above all other sources of instruction and development to man. Religion confers upon man eternal life and guides his footsteps in the world of morality. It opens the doors of unending happiness and bestows everlasting honor upon the human kingdom. It has been the basis of all civilization and progress in the history of mankind.

We will, therefore, investigate religion, seeking from an unprejudiced standpoint to discover whether it is the source of illumination, the cause of development and the animating impulse of all human advancement. We will investigate independently, free from the restrictions of dogmatic beliefs, blind imitations of ancestral forms and the influence of mere human opinion; for as we enter this question, we will find some who declare that religion is a cause of uplift and betterment in the world, while others assert just as positively that it is a detriment and a source of degradation to mankind. We must give these questions thorough and impartial consideration so that no doubt or uncertainty may linger in our minds regarding them.

How shall we determine whether religion has been the cause of human advancement or retrogression?

We will first consider the Founders of the religions—the Prophets—review the story of Their lives, compare the conditions preceding Their appearance with those subsequent to Their departure, following historical records and irrefutable facts instead of relying upon traditionary statements which are open to both acceptance and denial.

Among the great Prophets was Abraham, Who, being an iconoclast and a Herald of the oneness of God, was banished from His native land. He founded a family upon which the blessing of God descended, and it was owing to this religious basis and ordination that the Abrahamic house progressed and advanced. Through the divine benediction noteworthy and luminous prophets issued from His lineage. There appeared Isaac, Ishmael, Jacob, Joseph, Moses, Aaron, David and Solomon. The Holy Land was conquered by the power of the Covenant of God with Abraham, and the glory of the Solomonic wisdom and sovereignty dawned. All this was due to the religion of God which this blessed lineage established and upheld. It is evident that throughout the history of Abraham and His posterity this was the source of their honor, advancement and civilization. Even today the descendants of His household and lineage are found throughout the world.

There is another and more significant aspect to this religious impulse and impetus. The children of Israel were in bondage and captivity in the land of Egypt four hundred years. They were in an extreme state of degradation and slavery under the tyranny and oppression of the Egyptians. While they were in the condition of abject poverty, in the lowest degree of abasement, ignorance and servility, Moses suddenly appeared among them. Although He was but a shepherd, such majesty, grandeur and efficiency became manifest in Him through the power of religion that His influence continues to this day. His Prophethood was established throughout the land, and the law of His Word became the foundation of the laws of the nations. This unique Personage, single and alone, rescued the children of Israel from bondage through the power of religious training and discipline. He led them to the Holy Land and founded there a great civilization which has become permanent and renowned and under which these people attained the highest degree of honor and glory. He freed them from bondage and captivity. He imbued them with qualities of progressiveness and capability. They proved to be a civilizing people with instincts toward education and scholastic attainment. Their philosophy became renowned; their industries were celebrated throughout the nations. In all lines of advancement which characterize a progressive people they achieved distinction. In the splendor of the reign of Solomon their sciences and arts advanced to such a degree that even the Greek philosophers journeyed to Jerusalem to sit at the feet of the Hebrew sages and acquire the basis of Israelitish law. According to eastern history this is an established fact. Even Socrates visited the Jewish doctors in the Holy Land, consorting with them and discussing the principles and basis of their religious belief. After his return to Greece he formulated his philosophical teaching of divine unity and advanced his belief in the immortality of the spirit beyond the dissolution of the body. Without doubt, Socrates absorbed these verities from the wise men of the Jews with whom he came in contact. Hippocrates and other philosophers of the Greeks likewise visited Palestine and acquired wisdom from the Jewish prophets, studying the basis of ethics and morality, returning to their country with contributions which have made Greece famous.

When a movement fundamentally religious makes a weak nation strong, changes a nondescript tribal people into a mighty and powerful civilization, rescues them from captivity and elevates them to sovereignty, transforms their ignorance into knowledge and endows them with an impetus of advancement in all degrees of development (this is not theory, but historical fact), it becomes evident that religion is the cause of man's attainment to honor and sublimity.

But when we speak of religion, we mean the essential foundation or reality of religion, not the dogmas and blind imitations which have gradually encrusted it and which are the cause of the decline and effacement of a nation. These are inevitably destructive and a menace and hindrance to a nation's life—even as it is recorded in the *Torah* and confirmed in history that when the Jews became fettered by empty forms and imitations, the wrath of God became manifest. When they forsook the foundations of the law of God, Nebuchadnezzar came and conquered the Holy Land. He killed and made captive the people of Israel, laid waste the country and populous cities and burned the villages. Seventy thousand Jews were carried away captive to Babylon. He destroyed Jerusalem, despoiled the great Temple, desecrated the Holy of Holies and burned the *Torah*, the heavenly book of Scriptures. Therefore, we learn that allegiance to the essential foundation of the divine religions is ever the cause of development and progress, whereas the abandonment and beclouding of that essential reality through blind imitations and adherence to dogmatic beliefs are the causes of a nation's debasement and degradation. After their conquest by the Babylonians the Jews were successively subjugated by the Greeks and Romans. Under the Roman general Titus in A.D. 70 the Holy Land was stripped and pillaged, Jerusalem razed to its foundations and the Israelites scattered broadcast throughout the world. So complete was their dispersion that they have continued without a country and government of their own to the present day.

From this review of the history of the Jewish people we learn that the foundation of the religion of God laid by

Moses was the cause of their eternal honor and national prestige, the animating impulse of their advancement and racial supremacy and the source of that excellence which will always command the respect and reverence of those who understand their peculiar destiny and outcome. The dogmas and blind imitations which gradually obscured the reality of the religion of God proved to be Israel's destructive influences, causing the expulsion of these chosen people from the Holy Land of their Covenant and promise.

What, then, is the mission of the divine Prophets? Their mission is the education and advancement of the world of humanity. They are the real Teachers and Educators, the universal Instructors of mankind. If we wish to discover whether any one of these great Souls or Messengers was in reality a Prophet of God, we must investigate the facts surrounding His life and history, and the first point of our investigation will be the education He bestowed upon mankind. If He has been an Educator, if He has really trained a nation or people, causing it to rise from the lowest depths of ignorance to the highest station of knowledge, then we are sure that He was a Prophet. This is a plain and clear method of procedure, proof that is irrefutable. We do not need to seek after other proofs. We do not need to mention miracles, saying that out of rock water gushed forth, for such miracles and statements may be denied and refused by those who hear them. The deeds of Moses are conclusive evidences of His Prophethood. If a man be fair, unbiased and willing to investigate reality, he will undoubtedly testify to the fact that Moses was, verily, a man of God and a great Personage.

In further consideration of this subject, I wish you to be fair and reasonable in your judgment, setting aside all religious prejudices. We should earnestly seek and thoroughly investigate realities, recognizing that the

purpose of the religion of God is the education of humanity
and the unity and fellowship of mankind. Furthermore,
we will establish the point that the foundations of the
religions of God are one foundation. This foundation is
not multiple, for it is reality itself. Reality does not admit
of multiplicity, although each of the divine religions is
separable into two divisions. One concerns the world of
morality and the ethical training of human nature. It is
directed to the advancement of the world of humanity in
general; it reveals and inculcates the knowledge of God
and makes possible the discovery of the verities of life. This
is ideal and spiritual teaching, the essential quality of divine
religion, and not subject to change or transformation. It is
the one foundation of all the religions of God. Therefore,
the religions are essentially one and the same.

The second classification or division comprises social laws
and regulations applicable to human conduct. This is not
the essential spiritual quality of religion. It is subject to
change and transformation according to the exigencies and
requirements of time and place. For instance, in the time
of Noah certain requirements made it necessary that all
seafood be allowable or lawful. During the time of the
Abrahamic Prophethood it was considered allowable,
because of a certain exigency, that a man should marry his
aunt, even as Sarah was the sister of Abraham's mother.
During the cycle of Adam it was lawful and expedient for
a man to marry his own sister, even as Abel, Cain and
Seth, the sons of Adam, married their sisters. But in the
law of the Pentateuch revealed by Moses these marriages
were forbidden and their custom and sanction abrogated.
Other laws formerly valid were annulled during the time
of Moses. For example, it was lawful in Abraham's cycle to
eat the flesh of the camel, but during the time of Jacob this
was prohibited. Such changes and transformations in the

teaching of religion are applicable to the ordinary conditions of life, but they are not important or essential. Moses lived in the wilderness of Sinai where crime necessitated direct punishment. There were no penitentiaries or penalties of imprisonment. Therefore, according to the exigency of the time and place it was a law of God that an eye should be given for an eye and a tooth for a tooth. It would not be practicable to enforce this law at the present time—for instance, to blind a man who accidentally blinded you. In the *Torah* there are many commands concerning the punishment of a murderer. It would not be allowable or possible to carry out these ordinances today. Human conditions and exigencies are such that even the question of capital punishment—the one penalty which most nations have continued to enforce for murder—is now under discussion by wise men who are debating its advisability. In fact, laws for the ordinary conditions of life are only valid temporarily. The exigencies of the time of Moses justified cutting off a man's hand for theft, but such a penalty is not allowable now. Time changes conditions, and laws change to suit conditions. We must remember that these changing laws are not the essentials; they are the accidentals of religion. The essential ordinances established by a Manifestation of God are spiritual; they concern moralities, the ethical development of man and faith in God. They are ideal and necessarily permanent— expressions of the one foundation and not amenable to change or transformation. Therefore, the fundamental basis of the revealed religion of God is immutable, unchanging throughout the centuries, not subject to the varying conditions of the human world.

Christ ratified and proclaimed the foundation of the law of Moses. Muhammad and all the Prophets have revoiced that same foundation of reality. Therefore, the purposes and accomplishments of the divine Messengers have been one and the same. They were the source of advancement to the body politic and the cause of the honor and divine civilization of humanity, the foundation of which is one and the same in every dispensation. It is evident, then, that the proofs of the validity and inspiration of a Prophet of God are the deeds of beneficent accomplishment and greatness emanating from Him. If He proves to be instrumental in the elevation and betterment of mankind, He is undoubtedly a valid and heavenly Messenger. I wish you to be reasonable and just in your consideration of the following statements:

At the time when the Israelites had been dispersed by the power of the Roman Empire and the national life of the Hebrew people had been effaced by their conquerors—when the law of God had seemingly passed from them and the foundation of the religion of God was apparently destroyed—Jesus Christ appeared. When He arose among the Jews, the first thing He did was to proclaim the validity of the Manifestation of Moses. He declared that the *Torah*, the *Old Testament*, was the Book of God and that all the prophets of Israel were valid and true. He extolled the mission of Moses, and through His proclamation the name of Moses was spread throughout the world. Through Christianity the greatness of Moses became known among all nations. It is a fact that before the appearance of Christ, the name of Moses had not been heard in Persia. In India they had no knowledge of Judaism, and it was only through the Christianizing of Europe that the teachings of the *Old Testament* became spread in that region. Throughout Europe there was not a copy of the *Old Testament*. But consider this carefully and judge it aright: Through the instrumentality of Christ, through the translation of the *New Testament*, the little volume of the *Gospel*, the *Old Testament*, the *Torah*, has been translated into six hundred languages and spread everywhere in the world. The names of the Hebrew prophets became household words among the nations, who believed that the children of Israel were, verily, the chosen people of God, a holy nation under the especial blessing and protection of God, and that, therefore, the prophets who had arisen in Israel were the daysprings of revelation and brilliant stars in the heaven of the will of God.

Therefore, Christ really promulgated Judaism; for he was a Jew and not opposed to the Jews. He did not deny the Prophethood of Moses; on the contrary, He proclaimed and ratified it. He did not invalidate the *Torah*; He spread its teachings. That portion of the ordinances of Moses which concerned transactions and unimportant conditions underwent transformation, but the essential teachings of Moses were revoiced and confirmed by Christ without change. He left nothing unfinished or incomplete. Likewise, through the supreme efficacy and power of the Word of God He united most of the nations of the East and the West. This was accomplished at a time when these nations were opposed to each other in hostility and strife. He led them beneath the overshadowing tent of the oneness of humanity. He educated them until they became united and agreed, and through His spirit of conciliation the Roman, Greek, Chaldean and Egyptian were blended in a composite civilization. This wonderful power and extraordinary efficacy of the Word prove conclusively the validity of Christ. Consider how His heavenly sovereignty is still permanent and lasting. Verily, this is conclusive proof and manifest evidence.

From another horizon we see Muhammad, the Prophet of Arabia, appearing. You may not know that the first address of Muhammad to His tribe was the statement, "Verily, Moses was a Prophet of God, and the *Torah* is a Book of

God. Verily, O ye people, ye must believe in the *Torah*, in Moses and the prophets. Ye must accept all the prophets of Israel as valid." In the *Qur'an*, the Muslim Bible, there are seven statements or repetitions of the Mosaic narrative, and in all the historic accounts Moses is praised. Muhammad announces that Moses was the greatest Prophet of God, that God guided Him in the wilderness of Sinai, that through the light of guidance Moses hearkened to the summons of God, that He was the Interlocutor of God and the bearer of the tablet of the Ten Commandments, that all the contemporary nations of the world arose against Him and that eventually Moses conquered them, for falsehood and error are ever overcome by truth. There are many other instances of Muhammad's confirmation of Moses. I am mentioning but a few. Consider that Muhammad was born among the savage and barbarous tribes of Arabia, lived among them and was outwardly illiterate and uninformed of the Holy Books of God. The Arabian people were in the utmost ignorance and barbarism. They buried their infant daughters alive, considering this to be an evidence of a valorous and lofty nature. They lived in bondage and serfdom under the Persian and Roman governments and were scattered throughout the desert, engaged in continual strife and bloodshed. When the light of Muhammad dawned, the darkness of ignorance was dispelled from the deserts of Arabia. In a short period of time those barbarous peoples attained a superlative degree of civilization which, with Baghdad as its center, extended as far westward as Spain and afterward influenced the greater part of Europe. What proof of Prophethood could be greater than this, unless we close our eyes to justice and remain obstinately opposed to reason?

Today the Christians are believers in Moses, accept Him as a Prophet of God and praise Him most highly. The Muslims are, likewise, believers in Moses, accept the validity of His Prophethood, at the same time believing in Christ. Could it be said that the acceptance of Moses by the Christians and Muslims has been harmful and detrimental to those people? On the contrary, it has been beneficial to them, proving that they have been fair-minded and just. What harm could result to the Jewish people, then, if they in return should accept Christ and acknowledge the validity of the Prophethood of Muhammad? By this acceptance and praiseworthy attitude the enmity and hatred which have afflicted mankind so many centuries would be dispelled, fanaticism and bloodshed pass away and the world be blessed by unity and agreement. Christians and Muslims believe and admit that Moses was the Interlocutor of God. Why do you not say that Christ was the Word of God? Why do you not speak these few words that will do away with all this difficulty? Then there will be no more hatred and fanaticism, no more warfare and bloodshed in the Land of Promise. Then there will be peace among you forever.

Verily, I now declare to you that Moses was the Interlocutor of God and a most noteworthy Prophet, that Moses revealed the fundamental law of God and founded the real ethical basis of the civilization and progress of humanity. What harm is there in this? Have I lost anything by saying this to you and believing it as a Bahá'í? On the contrary, it benefits me; and Bahá'u'lláh, the Founder of the Bahá'í Movement, confirms me, saying, "You have been fair and just in your judgment; you have impartially investigated the truth and arrived at a true conclusion; you have announced your belief in Moses, a Prophet of God, and accepted the *Torah*, the Book of God." Inasmuch as it is possible for me to sweep away all evidences of prejudice by such a liberal and universal statement of belief, why is it not possible for you to do likewise? Why not put an end to this religious strife and establish a bond of connection between the hearts of men? Why should not the followers of one religion praise the Founder or Teacher of another? The other religionists extol the greatness of Moses and admit that He was the Founder of Judaism. Why do the Hebrews refuse to praise and accept the other great Messengers Who have appeared in the world? What harm could there be in this? What rightful objection? None whatever. You would lose nothing by such action and statement. On the contrary, you would contribute to the welfare of mankind. You would be instrumental in establishing the happiness of the world of humanity. The eternal honor of man depends upon the liberalism of this modern age. Inasmuch as our God is one God and the Creator of all mankind, He provides for and protects all. We acknowledge Him as a God of kindness, justice and mercy. Why then should we, His children and followers, war and fight, bringing sorrow and grief into the hearts of each other? God is loving and merciful. His intention in religion has ever been the bond of unity and affinity between humankind.

Praise be to God! The medieval ages of darkness have passed away and this century of radiance has dawned, this century wherein the reality of things is becoming evident, wherein science is penetrating the mysteries of the universe, the oneness of the world of humanity is being established, and service to mankind is the paramount motive of all existence. Shall we remain steeped in our fanaticisms and cling to our prejudices? Is it fitting that we should still be bound and restricted by ancient fables and superstitions of the past, be handicapped by superannuated beliefs and the ignorances of dark ages, waging religious wars, fighting and shedding blood, shunning and anathematizing each other? Is this becoming? Is it not better for us to be loving and considerate toward each other? Is it not preferable to

enjoy fellowship and unity, join in anthems of praise to
the most high God and extol all His Prophets in the spirit
of acceptance and true vision? Then, indeed, this world
will become a paradise, and the promised Day of God will
dawn. Then, according to the prophecy of Isaiah, the wolf
and the lamb will drink from the same stream, the owl and
the vulture will nest together in the same branches, and
the lion and the calf pasture in the same meadow. What
does this mean? It means that fierce and contending
religions, hostile creeds and divergent beliefs will reconcile
and associate, notwithstanding their former hatreds and
antagonism. Through the liberalism of human attitude
demanded in this radiant century they will blend together
in perfect fellowship and love. This is the spirit and meaning
of Isaiah's words. There will never be a day when this
prophecy will come to pass literally, for these animals by
their natures cannot mingle and associate in kindness and
love. Therefore, this prophecy symbolizes the unity and
agreement of races, nations and peoples who will come
together in attitudes of intelligence, illumination and
spirituality.

The age has dawned when human fellowship will become
a reality.

The century has come when all religions shall be unified.

The dispensation is at hand when all nations shall enjoy
the blessings of international peace.

The cycle has arrived when racial prejudice will be
abandoned by tribes and peoples of the world.

The epoch has begun wherein all native lands will be
conjoined in one great human family.

For all mankind shall dwell in peace and security beneath
the shelter of the great tabernacle of the one living God.[53]

'Abdu'l-Bahá

17

Christianity

Sacrifice and Original Sin

Thousands of years ago as mankind sought to develop an understanding of its place in creation, it gradually became clear that some higher power was at work. Forced to explain natural disasters, lightening, thunder, severe weather, accidents, eclipses and other such phenomenon, people began to believe there were gods who were somehow displeased with their actions. In order to placate these gods, peace offerings and sacrifices were performed on a regular basis. This practice developed independently in various cultures throughout the world.

Even when a single omnipotent God was the object of worship, oblations were a central aspect of worship, as were the priests who carried them out. Throughout the *Torah*, a great deal of attention is paid to peace offerings, burnt offerings, and sacrifices unto the Lord. Then in the *Book of Isaiah* the Lord speaks through the Prophet:

> To what purpose is the multitude of your sacrifices unto me? saith the Lord: I am full of the burnt offerings of rams, and the fat of fed beasts; and I delight not in the blood of bullocks, or of lambs, or of he goats. When ye come to appear before me, who hath required this at your hand, to tread my courts?[54]

Instead of making offerings, God commands them to, "cease to do evil; learn to do well; seek judgment, relieve the oppressed." Yet the allure of sacrifice for appeasement remained strong. In the *New Testament* Jesus is referred to as the lamb of God who would take away the sins of the world. Indeed, as we have seen, when a Prophet challenges the accepted ancestral beliefs and attracts followers, this incites the wrath of the religious establishment. Jesus surely sacrificed His life to allow mankind to become spiritually reborn, avoid sin, and live in a spirit of brotherly love. Others, however, see His sacrifice in a different context.

Although it is not found in the *Bible*, Christian theology teaches the concept of original sin, which is based upon the premise that everyone born into the world inherits the sins of his or her ancestors going back to Adam and Eve. According to church dogma, God sacrificed His only begotten Son to wash away mankind's original sins, and the only way to escape damnation is to accept Jesus Christ as one's personal saviour. Thus Christian dogma has elevated sacrifice to an unsurpassable level. Inasmuch as dogma maintains that Jesus is God incarnate, we have a situation in which God was sacrificed to God to wash away the sins of mankind.

I well recall being taught this as a child in Sunday School and asking about people who had never heard of Jesus. The teacher replied that it was unfortunate, but according to the *Bible* they could not be saved. To my young mind this did not ring true, nor as an adult can I accept that Jesus, the embodiment of love and compassion, Who forgave those who crucified Him, "because they know not what they do", could have sanctioned the punishment of those who did not have the opportunity to hear His message.

The *New Testament* was not written in Aramaic which Jesus spoke, rather it was recorded in Greek, beginning a few decades after His ascension and continuing perhaps for one hundred and twenty more years. Elaborate theologies based upon second and third hand accounts which were recorded in a second language decades later should be very carefully considered with the heart and the head. It is not my intention to imply that the *New Testament* is inaccurate, rather to suggest that we should concentrate on the spirit and not the letter of His message.

When I read the words attributed to Jesus in the *New Testament* it is clear that Jesus repeatedly alluded to the spiritual rebirth of mankind, and not to His own origins. He was born a living and breathing man, but reborn as the Spirit of God. He must have told His disciples of His spiritual awakening because it is recorded:

> And Jesus, when he was baptized, went up straightway out of the water: and, lo, the heavens were opened unto him, and he saw the Spirit of God descending like a dove, and lighting upon him.[55]

Later when He returned home and spoke at the local synagogue, the Jesus whom the townspeople had known no longer existed, He had been spiritually reborn. In the *Book of Matthew* their reaction is recorded:

> Is not this the carpenter's son? Is not his mother called Mary? And his brethren, James, and Joses, and Simon, and Judas? And his sisters, are they not all with us? Whence then hath this man all these things? And they were offended in him. But Jesus said unto them, a prophet is not without honour, save in his own country, and in his own house. And he did not many mighty works there because of their unbelief.[56]

Jesus taught that when a person is born of the spirit, he or she becomes a child of God, our heavenly Father. Once this rebirth takes place we become members of a spiritual family. Clearly, as it is recorded in the *Gospel of Mark*, Jesus neither placed importance on His material birth nor on His family:

> There came then his brethren and his mother, and, standing
> without, sent unto him, calling him. And the multitude
> sat about him, and they said unto him, behold, thy mother
> and thy brethren without seek for thee. And he answered
> them, saying, Who is my mother, or my brethren?

> And he looked round about on them which sat about him,
> and said, behold my mother and my brethren! For
> whosoever shall do the will of God, the same is my brother,
> and my sister, and mother.[57]

There is no denying that Jesus spoke often of His Father, and
referred to Himself as the Son of God. Still, we should not forget
that Jesus taught by means of allegories and parables, and we
cannot ignore that He also spoke to His followers as sons of
God.

> And call no man your father upon the earth: for one is
> your Father, which is in heaven.[58]

> I ascend unto my Father, and your Father; and to my God,
> and your God.[59]

> But if ye do not forgive, neither will your Father which is
> in heaven forgive your trespasses.[60]

> Be ye therefore merciful, as your Father also is merciful.[61]

> For it is not ye that speak, but the Spirit of your Father
> which speaketh in you.[62]

As for His death, Jesus began His mission fully aware of the
price He would pay for confronting the religious authorities of
His day. He knew He would sacrifice His life when He
announced He was the Word of God. If a Christian chooses to
believe that he is burdened with the sins of his ancestors, and
Christ died to wash them away, that is a matter of conscience.
He should not judge others for following their heart if it leads
them in another direction.

Although I was taught to believe in original sin, I have come to believe that each person is responsible for his own sins. I believe Christ sacrificed His life, not for our original sins, but to teach us how to live according to God's spiritual law. He sacrificed Himself to deliver a message of spiritual rebirth, love, compassion, and fellowship, and He called upon mankind to accent the spirit rather than the letter of the law. He died in order to summon mankind to embrace belief in the One True God. He died to call upon humanity to practise universal brotherly love. He sacrificed Himself to teach us how to avoid sin by living according to the Word of God which He embodied.

You might be asking yourself what original sin has to do with fanaticism. Let us recall how fanatically this dogma was defended in the past. Four hundred years ago the church would have had me burned alive for writing these lines. Even today Christian missionaries and television evangelists, often woefully uninformed of other religions, confidently judge and proclaim those who do not accept their particular interpretation of the Gospels as lost souls. This is a source of needless friction and enmity which does not reflect the mercy and compassion of Christ's message.

> Jesus Christ endured affliction and accepted martyrdom upon the cross in order to summon mankind to unity and love. What sacrifice could be greater? He brought the religion of love and fellowship into the world.[63]
>
> *'Abdu'l-Bahá*

The Challenge of Islam

Muhammad, like Jesus, retreated into the wilderness to meditate and cleanse Himself spiritually, and similarly the heavenly spirit descended upon Him. Since he was born of the spirit He unreservedly recognised Jesus as the Spirit of God and the Word of God. He taught His followers to believe likewise. Jesus taught, "Whosoever shall do the will of God, the same is my brother," and Muhammad taught, "Those who believe in God, and hold fast unto Him, them He will cause to enter into His mercy and grace, and will guide them unto Him by a straight road."

To those Jews who did not recognise His station Jesus said:

> If God were your Father, ye would love me: for I proceeded forth and came from God; neither came I of myself, but he sent me.[64]

To the Christians, Muhammad said:

> O ye people of the Book! our Apostle has come to you to explain to you much of what ye had hidden of the Book, and to pardon much. There has come to you from God a light, and a perspicuous Book; God guides thereby those who follow His pleasure to the way of peace, and brings them into a right way.[65]

Franklin Graham is one of the most influential Christian leaders in the United States today. He delivered the benediction at the inauguration of President George W. Bush and he is the son of the Reverend Billy Graham, the most well-known Christian evangelist of the twentieth century. In the November of 2001, Franklin Graham labelled the Islamic faith as, "wicked, violent and not of the same God."[66]

Many were quite surprised by his remarks, especially in light of Christ's command not to judge others:

> Judge not, and ye shall not be judged: condemn not, and ye shall not be condemned: forgive, and ye shall be forgiven.[67]

Jesus Himself was utterly magnanimous, when His disciples complained that another was acting in His name without following Him, Jesus told them to leave the man alone, "he that is not against us is for us." He stressed that we should be humble with respect to our faith:

Two men went up into the temple to pray; the one a
Pharisee, and the other a publican. The Pharisee stood and
prayed thus with himself, God, I thank thee, that I am not
as other men are, extortioners, unjust, adulterers, or even
as this publican. I fast twice in the week, I give tithes of all
that I possess. And the publican, standing afar off, would
not lift up so much as his eyes unto heaven, but smote
upon his breast, saying, God be merciful to me a sinner. I
tell you, this man went down to his house justified rather
than the other: for every one that exalteth himself shall be
abased; and he that humbleth himself shall be exalted.[68]

My heart tells me that Jesus would consider Hinduism,
Buddhism, and Zoroastianism religions which developed
independently and prior to His appearance, as "not against us"
and thus "for us". Clearly Islam, as Muhammad taught it,
venerates Jesus Christ and praises God.

Today, there are over a billion Muslims who, if they follow
the teachings of Muhammad, love and revere Jesus Christ. The
contention that they are not of the same God is untenable. The
Beneficent Merciful God of the *Qur'án* is clearly the Most High
God of the *Torah*, and the Heavenly Father of the *New Testament*.
He is the Omnipotent, All-Knowing, Creator of the Universe,
of Whom Jesus said: "Why callest thou me good? there is none
good but one, that is, God." Of Whom Muhammad taught:

In the name of God, the Beneficent, the Merciful. All that
is in the Heavens and all that is in the earth glorifieth God,
the Sovereign Lord, the Holy One, the Mighty, the Wise.[69]

Say: I am only a mortal like you. My Lord inspireth in me
that your God is only One God. And whoever hopeth for
the meeting with his Lord, let him do righteous work, and
make none sharer of the worship due unto his Lord.[70]

Whosoever surrendereth his purpose to God while doing good, he verily hath grasped the firm hand-hold. Unto God belongeth the sequel of all things.[71]

There are Christian evangelists and missionaries who entertain an unrealistic vision of a mass conversion of Muslims to Christianity. This is no more likely than a mass conversion of Christians to Judaism. There is no logical reason to give up something you cherish in order to obtain something which you already have. Moreover, Christians might reflect that Jews and Muslims practise a straightforward and unequivocal monotheism which shuns graven images and pictures in temples or mosques. No Muslim would ever consider portraying Muhammad or God with an image, yet the Catholic church even commissioned paintings which portray God as a man with a long white beard. Christians might try to imagine how certain Christian churches teeming with statues and pictures of saints and prominent clergymen appear to Jews and Muslims. The same holds true for the practice of praying to saints, or Mary, the mother of Jesus. To some Christians this seems perfectly natural, but for Jews and Muslims the focus of worship is God and God alone, they seek no intermediaries. Imagine what it is like for a Muslim to have such a Christian maintain that he worships a false god, and then seek to convert him without even understanding the true nature of Islam.

There was great wisdom in the fact that Muhammad did not claim to be the only way, and that He allowed Christians to continue to practise their religion. He did not predicate the salvation of Christians or Jews upon their acceptance of His Prophethood. This example of tolerance should be the basis for the peaceful coexistence of Jews, Christians, and Muslims. There was an implicit acknowledgement that Muhammad was called upon to minister to a distinct people. Up until then the Arabs had rejected Christianity and His message was clearly tailored to meet their circumstances.

Clearly, many of the stringent laws of Islam, once indispensable to establishing civil order and a just society, are no longer suitable for modern societies with secular governments. Thus, I am not making a case for Christians to become Muslims. Yet, it would unquestionably improve our world if Christians would recognise that Muhammad was a messenger of God Who ministered to a savage people in seventh century Arabia and enabled them to attain the heights of civilisation at a time in which Europe was stuck in the Dark Ages. Just as Muhammad recognised Christians as people of the book, Christians should see Muslims in the same light.

In the spirit of humility, Christians could also recognise that Muslims have achieved some things which Christians have not. If we had truly understood the parable of the Good Samaritan, racism among Christians would be unthinkable. Malcolm X, an African American scarred by racism, became a militant Black Muslim and a prominent spokesman for black separatism. Eventually, however, he became an orthodox Muslim and made a pilgrimage to Mecca. There his heart was changed by the true spirit of Islam. Here is a portion of a letter which he wrote from Mecca which shows that the power of God can also be seen in the fruits of Islam:

> There were tens of thousands of pilgrims, from all over the world. They were of all colors, from blue-eyed blonds to black skinned Africans. But we were all participating in the same ritual, displaying a spirit of unity and brotherhood that my experience in America had led me to believe never could exist between the white and the non-white.

> America needs to understand Islam, because this is the one religion that erases from its society the race problem...[72]

Christians wishing to understand Islam need to become acquainted with seventh century Arabia. Without this knowledge and an understanding of the treachery of various tribes who endangered the survival of the Muslim community, including Jews and disingenuous converts to Islam, isolated passages can appear brutal when read from the comfort of one's living room. Indeed, such passages are readily employed by Islam's detractors.

The tribes which Muhammad tamed were hardened and warlike and the *Qur'án* reflects that reality. The promises of rewards in the afterlife, used to subdue their brutality, are vivid and descriptive, as are the punishments employed for the same purpose. Moses was confronted with a similar group and we know from the *Book of Exodus* the many crimes which were punishable by death, for example breaking the Sabbath:

> Six days may work be done; but in the seventh is the sabbath of rest, holy to the Lord: whosoever doeth any work in the sabbath day, he shall surely be put to death.[73]

Muhammad's message was well-suited to the tribes of Arabia, as was Moses' to the tribes of Israel, and it is important to understand the *Qur'án* in that context. Without going into too much detail, the *Qur'án* can be divided into two very broad categories, the Mecca period, and the Medina period. During the Mecca period, Muhammad was a preacher who admonished the brutal, drunken, idolaters of Mecca. During the Medina period He was a nation builder, responsible for protecting His followers from murderous tribes bent on their destruction. Far from being a bloodthirsty warmonger, it is recorded in the *Qur'án* that He hated war but had no other choice in dealing with those seeking the annihilation of the Muslim community. His defence of His followers and the taming of Arabia against staggering odds was nothing short of miraculous.

His capacity to forgive, little known in the West, was repeatedly demonstrated. For example, after the taking of Mecca where He had endured such severe persecution, He simply destroyed the idols and, to the surprise of the populace, proclaimed a general amnesty. Another instance would be when He was poisoned. On that occasion, one of His companions died upon eating poisoned meat, and although Muhammad did not swallow, by merely tasting it He became gravely ill. When the Jewish woman who prepared the meat was brought before Him, He asked her why she did it. She replied that it was because her people had been humiliated, and He promptly forgave her.

Muhammad's son-in-law, the Imam Ali, was also the son of His uncle and one of the first to declare his belief in Muhammad. He was one of Muhammad's closest and most trusted followers. When Muhammad fled Mecca as the tribes plotted to murder him at His home, it was Ali who put on His robes to lie on His bed so they would think Muhammad was still in Mecca. Ali was the last Muslim to leave Mecca. This is how he remembered Muhammad:

> He was of the middle height, neither very tall nor very short. His skin was fair but ruddy, His eyes black; His beard, that surrounded all His face, luxuriant. The hair of His head was long and fell to His shoulders; it was black. His neck was white... His gait was so energetic you would have said He was wrenching His foot from a stone, yet at the same time so light He seemed to float... But He did not walk with pride, as the princes do. There was such sweetness in His face, that once you were in His presence you could not leave Him; if you were hungry, it fed you just to look at Him... When they entered His presence, the afflicted forgot their anguish. Whoever saw Him declared that he had never found, before or afterward, a man of such entrancing speech. His nose was aquiline, His teeth somewhat far apart. Sometimes He would let His hair fall free, sometimes He wore it knotted in two or four strands.

At sixty-three... age had whitened but some fifteen of His hairs...[74]

In order to gain an appreciation of Muhammad in the same way that a Christian might Jesus, it is necessary to read the *Hadith*. The *Hadith* is a collection of traditions, or witnessed accounts, which reveal Muhammad's standard of living faith, referred to by Muslims as His Sunna (example). In the *Hadith* we discover a warm, peace-loving, tolerant and wise leader Who embodied spirituality and virtue.

Christ taught us to be meek, merciful, humble, loving, pure in heart, and peacemakers. He guided us to be mindful of our own shortcomings and non-judgemental towards others. At this particular point in time, extremists who claim to act in the name of Islam give Christians an opportunity to put these tenets of their faith to the test. We must recognise that not everyone who calls himself a Muslim embodies the teachings of Muhammad.

From our own dark history in Europe and America we know what was done by professed Christians—at times in the name of God. These transgressions are not limited to the distant past. There was the ethnic cleansing of Muslims in the Balkans in the 1990's. African American churches in America were burned and bombed by self-professed Christians who hid behind hoods, and burned crosses to terrorise those who looked and believed differently. Adolf Hitler did not act alone. Virtually everyone who supported him had been baptised and confirmed and was a Christian in name. Six million European Jews were forced into slave labour and then systematically killed. Afterwards their hair was used to stuff mattresses, their skin was used for lampshades, and their teeth were ripped out in order to salvage their gold fillings. It is difficult to think of a more cynical and despicable display of man's inhumanity to man. Rightfully Christians understand that these actions are an anathema to

Christ's teachings. It should, however, cause us to be very humble in our approach to other religions.

There are over a billion Muslims in the world, around a billion Hindus, and there are hundreds of millions of Buddhists in the world. Christ called upon Christians to be humble peacemakers, but as we have seen by the comments of Franklin Graham, Christian leaders sometimes sow the seeds of discord instead of the message of peace and understanding. Pat Robertson is a prominent television evangelist, the founder of the Christian Broadcasting Network, and host of the "700 Club" seen in over eighty countries. In 1991, he released a book entitled, *The New World Order*, in which he warned of the dangers of a unified world. In it he wrote, "The Allah of the Muslims is not the God of Jacob."[75] He also wrote, "If anybody understood what Hindus really believe, there would be no doubt that they have no business administering government policies in a country that favours freedom and equality."[76]

These kinds of smug denunciations foster an impression of arrogance and pride, the very things of which Christ warned. We do not glorify Christ or God by demeaning or maligning other faiths. Christians who accept the Bahá'í teachings recognise there is a clear wisdom, indeed a necessity that the Bahá'í Faith builds upon the foundation of Islam, and Bahá'ís recognise and revere equally the founders of all the world religions. Only through a change of heart will the wolf and the lamb feed together, and the lion eat straw like a bull. Please refer to the appendix on the Bahá'í Faith and Christianity for more on this topic.

As a young man I became a member of the Bahá'í Faith, a religion which has endured extreme persecution at the hands of Muslims. The Báb, Who like John the Baptist appeared and announced the coming of One greater than Himself, was killed by a firing squad in 1850 in Persia. Bahá'u'lláh, of Whom the Báb spoke, was tortured, imprisoned and eventually exiled to the penal colony of Akka, in what is today Israel. In Persia, during the nineteenth century, twenty thousand of their followers were killed for refusing to recant their beliefs. Even today in Iran, Bahá'ís continue to be denied religious and civil liberties, and human rights organisations have documented violations ranging from the execution of Bahá'ís to the denial of education to Bahá'í children. Although the persecution of Bahá'ís is most widespread in Iran, they have also suffered in other Islamic nations. Yet over the course of my adult life, I have found myself repeatedly defending Muhammad and the faith of Islam.

Fareed Zakaria, a Muslim journalist, wrote in *Newsweek* magazine:

> Nothing will be solved by searching for "true Islam" or quoting the Quran. The Quran is a vast, vague book, filled with poetry and contradictions (much like the Bible). You can find in it condemnations of war and incitements to struggle, beautiful expressions of tolerance and stern

strictures against unbelievers. Quotations from it usually tell us more about the person who selected the passages than about Islam.[77]

As a Bahá'í, I concentrate on the beautiful spiritual message of Islam and view the calls to struggle and the rebuke of unbelievers within their historical context. For me a Muslim is someone who has surrendered his or her will to the will of our Merciful and Compassionate God, the Lord of All the Worlds. A true Muslim is engaged in a jihad for the conquest of his or her own selfishness and egotism, which Muhammad considered the holiest of struggles. This form of jihad requires introspection, honest reflection, and a critical personal inventory of one's strengths and weaknesses. It enjoins the individual to accept personal responsibility for mistakes and shortcomings. Especially in the light of recent events, Muslims as a community need to reflect upon their role in the world, and their relationship to our Merciful and Compassionate God.

Truth, Reason and Logic

Islam was once known for its tolerant and progressive civilisation. The Imam Ali taught that the ink of the scholar was holier than the blood of a martyr. Early generations of Muslims thirsted after knowledge and enlightenment, and they sought truth regardless of its origins. In the eighth and ninth centuries, the major works of ancient Greek philosophy were translated into Arabic and as a result of this stimulus the first major Islamic theological movement, the Mutazilites, was born. They venerated reason and observed rigorous logic in approaching the question of God, faith and religion. They championed the absolute unity of God, Whom they held to be an Indivisible Essence, the Ultimate Justice. They understood the individual must have free will, otherwise reward and punishment would be senseless. Consequently, they maintained that the individual bore the responsibility to choose between good and evil. They taught that human reason gave man the ability to distinguish between good and evil, but this ability was enhanced by knowledge of the holy scriptures.

The Caliph al-Mamun embraced and endorsed their theology, but by the tenth century, the acceptance of this enlightened theology waned after it was denounced by the philosopher al-Ashari. He rejected the concept of free will because he considered it incompatible with God's will and absolute power. Further, he rejected the idea that man possesses the ability to discern good and evil on his own, he argued that this knowledge was only given through scripture. Al-Ashari's views gradually became predominant among followers of the Sunni branch of Islam, who make up the majority of the Muslim community.

Doubting the power of human reason ignores a significant fact, the human mind is a gift given to man by God, and that is why man can discern right from wrong, and good from evil. Had the Islamic community remained firmly committed to placing trust in human reason, logic, and the search for truth wherever it might lead, it seems likely that today the Islamic nations would be the envy of the world.

Adapting to Circumstances

Admittedly, no one can deny that Muslims and Islamic nations have suffered injustices at the hands of Western powers throughout the course of history. However, Christians have also suffered at the hands of other Christians, and Muslims have suffered injustices at the hands of other Muslims. The hallmark of prejudice is the inability to see people as unique individuals. If, for example, a Frenchman were robbed and beaten by another Frenchman, he would not spend the rest of his life hating Frenchmen. But if he were robbed and beaten by a member of another race or ethnic group, there is a real possibility that he would harbour resentment against the entire group and pass this prejudice on to his children.

Thus Hindus do not hate Hindus, even though Gandhi was killed by a fanatical Hindu who considered him an agent of Islamic interests. Jews do not hate Jews because Yitzhak Rabin was murdered by a fanatical Jew who wanted to stop the peace process. Muslims do not hate Muslims because Egyptian President Anwar Sadat was killed by fanatical Muslims for making peace with Israel in exchange for land, and for supporting a secular government in Egypt. Similarly, for many Muslims the Iran/Iraq war, in which a million Muslims were killed by fellow Muslims, is easily forgotten, but each and every injustice associated with "unbelievers" is a source of outrage which demands revenge. For many people, the ethnic killings of 800,000 Tutsis and moderate Hutus in Central Africa, because it was not black against white, did not resonate as loudly as the injustice of apartheid in South Africa. Finally, the brutal repression of woman in Afghanistan under the Taliban brought few cries of outrage in the Islamic world, but imagine the reaction if their tormentors had been Christians, Jews, or Hindus.

When we fixate on injustices (perpetrated by "others") which extend back over centuries or millennia, this inevitably leads to the emergence of feelings of victimisation, bitterness, and self-pity. Hatred, resentment and a longing for vengeance are understandable, but these negative emotions serve no one. A mind preoccupied with hate and bitterness cannot truly commune with God, thus Jesus counselled the individual to love his enemy, and Krishna taught we should hate no living creature. When we allow ourselves to give in to negative emotions like hate, this depletes us of spirituality and creative potential. The irony is that the person who hates is consumed with anger and resentment, while the progeny of the perceived offenders are often unaware of the hate directed at them. They move on with their lives, unaware of the hater's dark world, and channel their energies into positive pursuits.

We must ask ourselves, who benefits when we continually shift blame for past injustices onto the shoulders of the next generation? Learning to see people as unique individuals helps us to overcome prejudice. It also allows us to live in the present, a healthy psychological state, rather than dwelling in the past with feelings of anger and resentment. My point is not that one should ignore injustice, rather one should adapt to circumstances which are clearly beyond one's control, and react as positively as possible. For example, throughout European history the Jews suffered grave injustices and persecution and were barred from entry into trades and guilds. Their reaction was to embrace education and enter into professions. Jews became doctors, lawyers, bankers, academics, and scientists. Today, even though Germans systematically murdered six million Jews, their descendants are welcomed in Israel and the governments of the two nations enjoy amicable relations.

The case of Japan is another example of a positive reaction to circumstances beyond one's control. The U.S. officially entered the second World War when Japan destroyed much of the U.S. Pacific Fleet with a surprise attack on Pearl Harbour. Japanese forces simultaneously attacked British Malaya, Guam, the Philippines, Hong Kong, Midway Island, Thailand, and Wake Island. In the end, the U.S. destroyed two Japanese cities with atomic bombs to end the war and force Japan into an unconditional surrender.

Japan was stripped of its empire and an occupation force led by a U.S. general, and assisted by the Allied Council for Japan with representatives from China, U.S.S.R., and Great Britain, governed and reformed Japanese society. They quickly disestablished Shintoism as Japan's state religion and mandated religious freedom. Until then, Shintoism demanded that the emperor be worshipped as a god and asserted the racial superiority of the Japanese people. The emperor was also compelled to renounce all claims to divinity. The economy was reformed and industrial and banking trusts were broken. Land reforms were enacted which enabled tenant farmers to purchase the land they worked. A democratic form of government was mandated and the first post-war democratic election was held in 1946. Women were given the franchise to participate in politics and were elected into the first diet. Educational reforms encouraged self-expression, placed a new emphasis on social studies, and prohibited the spreading of nationalistic ideology. Eventually in 1951, a formal peace treaty was signed which restored Japan's sovereign rights, but mandated the presence of American security forces in Japan.

Certainly the Japanese could have found ample reasons to sink into state of anger, resentment and self-pity. Yet in general, they adapted to the changed circumstances and moved on with their lives. Western culture and methods which they found advantageous were embraced, while others were rejected and discarded. They chose to shape their destiny with sweat not tears. They rose mightily from those post-war years to become world leaders in several fields, and an important diplomatic and trading partner of their former enemies.

It takes maturity and humility to admit mistakes and accept personal responsibility. For an individual, and for a community, it is easier to avoid the pain of acknowledging mistakes by simply blaming others. In the *Qur'án*, however, Muslims are called upon to judge fairly:

> O ye who believe! be ye steadfast in justice, witnessing before God though it be against yourselves, or your parents, or your kindred, be it rich or poor, for God is nearer akin than either.

Muslims might consider whether their community actually benefits from avoiding critical self-examination. It is too simplistic to blame the lack of democracy and progress in Islamic societies solely on the West. Is it not possible that to some degree a contempt for the "infidel" has caused some Muslim communities to ignore Western ideas which could have bettered their living conditions? While Europeans profited greatly from adopting and adapting elements of Islamic civilisation, Muslim clerics have preached against adopting the practices of unbelievers. Clearly, Western culture brings with it many dangers and undesirable influences, but those Islamic clerics who are contemptuous of free will, human reason, self-determination, freedom of expression, progress, democracy, women, and unbelievers must bear some responsibility for the stagnation of Islamic civilisation and the ascendancy of the West.

In the Freedom House annual survey of freedom and democracy for the year 2001, three quarters of the nations of the world are classified as "free" or "partly free".[78] In Africa, the figure is sixty per cent, but in the Middle East only one-quarter (28%) of nations are deemed to be free or partly free. The people of the Middle East should recognise that fanaticism, militancy, and hardline fundamentalism are daunting obstacles which stand in the way of progress, democracy, and self-determination. Moreover, those who incite passions, hatred, and prejudice against Western democratic governments are the problem, not the solution.

Japan and Germany were once America's mortal enemies, yet after the second World War America played a dominant mentoring role in establishing democratic governments in both nations. Why is this not the case in the Middle East? As many analysts have pointed out, when free and democratic nations seek to pressure Middle Eastern governments to expand civil liberties, political freedom, and human rights, they are immediately rebuffed by these governments with the warning that to do so would bring chaos and the establishment of dangerously hostile hardline Islamic governments. They warn that the Western concept of "one person, one vote" would only work "one time" in the Middle East. They caution that once the Islamic extremists come to power, democracy will come to an end. With the world's dependence on imported oil and the possibility of a cataclysmic confrontation between Israel and Arab states, is it any wonder that democratic governments are restrained in their advocacy for democracy in the Middle East?

How does one adapt to these circumstances? It requires a seemingly contradictory approach. For the Middle East the door which leads to freedom, progress and integration into the global community is opened by pulling, not pushing. The harder you push, the tighter the door will shut. On the other hand, by rejecting fanaticism and militancy, while peacefully pursuing dialogue, you will remove the obstacles which stand in your way. The door which you seek to open will be opened by loyal, productive, and trustworthy citizens who possess the ability to compromise. This is how to adapt to circumstances, do not be swayed by fanatics.

'Abdu'l-Bahá made an impassioned plea to the people of Persia to reject fanaticism and embrace reason, knowledge, and the power of the human mind. His advice remains valid for the people of the Middle East today:

In the Name of God the Clement, the Merciful

Praise and thanksgiving be unto Providence that out of all the realities in existence He has chosen the reality of man and has honored it with intellect and wisdom, the two most luminous lights in either world...If we look objectively upon the world of being, it will become apparent that from age to age, the temple of existence has continually been embellished with a fresh grace, and distinguished with an ever-varying splendor, deriving from wisdom and the power of thought.

This supreme emblem of God stands first in the order of creation and first in rank, taking precedence over all created things. Witness to it is the Holy Tradition, "Before all else, God created the mind." From the dawn of creation, it was made to be revealed in the temple of man...

O ye that have minds to know! Raise up your suppliant hands to the heaven of the one God, and humble yourselves and be lowly before Him, and thank Him for this supreme endowment, and implore Him to succor us until, in this present age, godlike impulses may radiate from the conscience of mankind, and this divinely kindled fire which has been entrusted to the human heart may never die away.

Consider carefully: all these highly varied phenomena, these concepts, this knowledge, these technical procedures and philosophical systems, these sciences, arts, industries and inventions—all are emanations of the human mind. Whatever people has ventured deeper into this shoreless sea, has come to excel the rest. The happiness and pride of a nation consist in this, that it should shine out like the sun in the high heaven of knowledge. "Shall they who have knowledge and they who have it not, be treated alike?"[79] And the honor and distinction of the individual consist in this, that he among all the world's multitudes should become a source of social good. Is any larger bounty conceivable than this, that an individual, looking within himself, should find that by the confirming grace of God he has become the cause of peace and well-being, of happiness and advantage to his fellow men? No, by the one true God, there is no greater bliss, no more complete delight.

How long shall we drift on the wings of passion and vain desire; how long shall we spend our days like barbarians in the depths of ignorance and abomination? God has given

us eyes, that we may look about us at the world, and lay
hold of whatsoever will further civilization and the arts of
living. He has given us ears, that we may hear and profit
by the wisdom of scholars and philosophers and arise to
promote and practice it. Senses and faculties have been
bestowed upon us, to be devoted to the service of the general
good; so that we, distinguished above all other forms of
life for perceptiveness and reason, should labor at all times
and along all lines, whether the occasion be great or small,
ordinary or extraordinary, until all mankind are safely
gathered into the impregnable stronghold of knowledge.
We should continually be establishing new bases for human
happiness   and   creating   and   promoting   new
instrumentalities toward this end. How excellent, how
honorable is man if he arises to fulfil his responsibilities;
how wretched and contemptible, if he shuts his eyes to the
welfare of society and wastes his precious life in pursuing
his own selfish interests and personal advantages. Supreme
happiness is man's, and he beholds the signs of God in the
world and in the human soul, if he urges on the steed of
high endeavor in the arena of civilization and justice. "We
will surely show them Our signs in the world and within
themselves." [80]

...We must now highly resolve to arise and lay hold of all
those instrumentalities that promote the peace and well-
being and happiness, the knowledge, culture and industry,
the dignity, value and station, of the entire human race.
Thus, through the restoring waters of pure intention and
unselfish effort, the earth of human potentialities will
blossom with its own latent excellence and flower into
praiseworthy qualities, and bear and flourish until it comes
to rival that rosegarden of knowledge which belonged to
our forefathers. Then will this holy land of Persia become
in every sense the focal center of human perfections,

reflecting as if in a mirror the full panoply of world civilization.[81]

The state of Israel and America's dependence or foreign oil are often cited as a basis for the many of the problems in the Middle East. Yet long before the establishment of the state of Israel or the first barrel of oil was exported to America, Muslims in the Middle East were rejecting ideas which originated in the West. In 1875, 'Abdu'l-Bahá appealed to Muslims in the same book not to reject concepts like parliamentary government simply because they are common in the West. I ask you to consider his words with an eye towards justice:

> In the sign of Muhammad, the Sun of Truth rose over Yathrib (Medina) and the Hijáz and cast across the universe the lights of eternal glory. Then the earth of human potentialities was transformed, and the words "The earth shall shine with the light of her Lord," were fulfilled. The old world turned new again, and its dead body rose into abundant life. Then tyranny and ignorance were overthrown, and towering palaces of knowledge and justice were reared in their place. A sea of enlightenment thundered, and science cast down its rays. The savage peoples of the Hijáz, before that Flame of supreme Prophethood was lit in the lamp of Mecca, were the most brutish and benighted of all the peoples of the earth. In all the histories, their depraved and vicious practices, their ferocity and their constant feuds, are a matter of record... And yet, after the Light of the World rose over them, they were—because of the education bestowed on them by that Mine of perfections, that Focal Center of Revelation, and the blessings vouchsafed by the Divine Law—within a brief interval gathered into the shelter of the principle of Divine oneness. This brutish people then attained such a high degree of human perfection and civilization that all their contemporaries marveled at them. Those very peoples who

had always mocked the Arabs and held them up to ridicule as a breed devoid of judgment, now eagerly sought them out, visiting their countries to acquire enlightenment and culture, technical skills, statecraft, arts and sciences.

Observe the influence on material situations of that training which is inculcated by the true Educator. Here were tribes so benighted and untamed that during the period of the Jáhilíyyih they would bury their seven-year-old daughters alive—an act which even an animal, let alone a human being, would hate and shrink from but which they in their extreme degradation considered the ultimate expression of honor and devotion to principle—and this darkened people, thanks to the manifest teachings of that great Personage, advanced to such a degree that after they conquered Egypt, Syria and its capital Damascus, Chaldea, Mesopotamia and Iran, they came to administer single-handedly whatever matters were of major importance in four main regions of the globe.

The Arabs then excelled all the peoples of the world in science and the arts, in industry and invention, in philosophy, government and moral character. And truly, the rise of this brutish and despicable element, in such a short interval, to the supreme heights of human perfection, is the greatest demonstration of the rightfulness of the Lord Muhammad's Prophethood...

That Source of Divine wisdom, that Manifestation of Universal Prophethood (Muhammad), encouraging mankind to acquire sciences and arts and similar advantages has commanded them to seek these even in the furthermost reaches of China; yet the incompetent and caviling doctors (Muslim scholars) forbid this, offering as their justification the saying, "He who imitates a people is one of them." They have not even grasped what is meant by the "imitation" referred to, nor do they know that the Divine religions enjoin upon and encourage all the faithful to adopt such principles as will conduce to continuous improvements, and to acquire from other peoples sciences and arts. Whoever expresses himself to the contrary has never drunk of the nectar of knowledge and is astray in his own ignorance, groping after the mirage of his desires.

Judge this aright: which one of these modern developments, whether in themselves or in their application, is contrary to the Divine commandments? If they mean the establishment of parliaments, these are enjoined by the very text of the holy verse: "and whose affairs are guided by mutual counsel."

... Can we maintain that it is contrary to the fundamentals of the Faith to encourage the acquisition of useful arts and of general knowledge, to inform oneself as to the truths of such physical sciences as are beneficial to man, and to widen the scope of industry and increase the products of commerce and multiply the nation's avenues of wealth? Would it conflict with the worship of God to establish law and order in the cities and organize the rural districts, to repair the roads and build railroads and facilitate transportation and travel and thus increase the people's well-being? Would it be inconsistent with the Divine commands and prohibitions if we were to work the abandoned mines which are the greatest source of the nation's wealth, and to build factories, from which come the entire people's comfort, security and affluence? Or to stimulate the creation of new industries and to promote improvements in our domestic products?

By the All-Glorious! I am astonished to find what a veil has fallen across their eyes, and how it blinds them even to such obvious necessities as these. And there is no doubt whatever that when conclusive arguments and proofs of this sort are advanced, they will answer, out of a thousand hidden spites and prejudices: "On the Day of Judgment, when men stand before their Lord, they will not be questioned as to their education and the degree of their culture—rather will they be examined as to their good deeds." Let us grant this and assume that man will not be asked as to his culture and education; even so, on that great Day of Reckoning, will not the leaders be called to account? Will it not be said to them: "O chiefs and leaders! Why did ye cause this mighty nation to fall from the heights of its former glory, to pass from its place at the heart and center of the civilized world? Ye were well able to take hold of such measures as would lead to the high honor of this people. This ye failed to do, and ye even went on to deprive them of the common benefits enjoyed by all. Did not this people once shine out like stars in an auspicious heaven? How have ye dared to quench their light in darkness! Ye could have lit the lamp of temporal and eternal glory for them; why did ye fail to strive for this with all your hearts? And when by God's grace a flaming Light flared up, why did ye fail to shelter it in the glass of your valor, from the winds that beat against it? Why did ye rise up in all your might to put it out?"

Again, is there any deed in the world that would be nobler than service to the common good? Is there any greater blessing conceivable for a man, than that he should become the cause of the education, the development, the prosperity and honor of his fellow-creatures? No, by the Lord God! The highest righteousness of all is for blessed souls to take hold of the hands of the helpless and deliver them out of their ignorance and abasement and poverty, and with pure motives, and only for the sake of God, to arise and energetically devote themselves to the service of the masses, forgetting their own worldly advantage and working only to serve the general good. "They prefer them before themselves, though poverty be their own lot."[82] "The best of men are those who serve the people; the worst of men are those who harm the people."

Glory be to God! What an extraordinary situation now obtains, when no one, hearing a claim advanced, asks himself what the speaker's real motive might be, and what selfish purpose he might not have hidden behind the mask of words. You find, for example, that an individual seeking to further his own petty and personal concerns, will block the advancement of an entire people... To maintain his own leadership, he will everlastingly direct the masses toward that prejudice and fanaticism which subvert the very base of civilization.

Such a man, at the same moment that he is perpetrating actions which are anathema in the sight of God and detested by all the Prophets and Holy Ones, if he sees a person who has just finished eating wash his hands with soap—an article the inventor of which was 'Abdu'lláh Buní, a Muslim—will, because this unfortunate does not instead wipe his hands up and down the front of his robe and on his beard, set up a hue and cry to the effect that the religious law has been overthrown, and the manners and customs of heathen nations are being introduced into ours. Utterly disregarding the evil of his own ways, he considers the very cause of cleanliness and refinement as wicked and foolish.

O People of Persia! Open your eyes! Pay heed! Release yourselves from this blind following of the bigots, this senseless imitation which is the principal reason why men fall away into paths of ignorance and degradation. See the true state of things. Rise up; seize hold of such means as will bring you life and happiness and greatness and glory among all the nations of the world.

...The pure water of life is welling up, why wear away your days in a desert of thirst? Aim high, choose noble ends;

how long this lethargy, how long this negligence! Despair, both here and hereafter, is all you will gain from self-indulgence; abomination and misery are all you will harvest from fanaticism, from believing the foolish and the mindless. The confirmations of God are supporting you, the succor of God is at hand: why do you not cry out and exult with all your heart, and strive with all your soul!

Among those matters which require thorough revision and reform is the method of studying the various branches of knowledge and the organization of the academic curriculum... The individual should, prior to engaging in the study of any subject, ask himself what its uses are and what fruit and result will derive from it. If it is a useful branch of knowledge, that is, if society will gain important benefits from it, then he should certainly pursue it with all his heart. If not, if it consists in empty, profitless debates and in a vain concatenation of imaginings that lead to no result except acrimony, why devote one's life to such useless hairsplittings and disputes.

...The primary, the most urgent requirement is the promotion of education. It is inconceivable that any nation should achieve prosperity and success unless this paramount, this fundamental concern is carried forward. The principal reason for the decline and fall of peoples is ignorance. Today the mass of the people are uninformed even as to ordinary affairs, how much less do they grasp the core of the important problems and complex needs of the time...

It is, furthermore, a vital necessity to establish schools throughout Persia, even in the smallest country towns and villages, and to encourage the people in every possible way to have their children learn to read and write. If necessary, education should even be made compulsory. Until the nerves and arteries of the nation stir into life, every measure that is attempted will prove vain; for the people are as the human body, and determination and the will to struggle are as the soul, and a soulless body does not move. This dynamic power is present to a superlative degree in the very nature of the Persian people, and the spread of education will release it.

...Indeed, the majority of the reactionaries and the procrastinators are only concealing their own selfish interests under a barrage of idle words, and confusing the minds of the helpless masses with public statements which bear no relation to their well-concealed objectives.

O people of Persia! The heart is a divine trust; cleanse it from the stain of self-love, adorn it with the coronal of pure intent, until the sacred honor, the abiding greatness of this illustrious nation may shine out like the true morning in an auspicious heaven. This handful of days on earth will slip away like shadows and be over. Strive then that God may shed His grace upon you, that you may leave a favorable remembrance in the hearts and on the lips of those to come. "And grant that I be spoken of with honor by posterity."[83]

Happy the soul that shall forget his own good, and like the chosen ones of God, vie with his fellows in service to the good of all...[84]

One God and Two Classes of People?

Recently during a television discussion programme involving several prominent Muslims, a caller asked why all people can visit the holy sites of other religions, but only Muslims can visit Mecca. Although they surely knew the answer, none of the panellists offered an explanation. Previously, I pointed out that Muslims have been considerably more willing to overlook race in their dealings with fellow believers than is the case with

Christians. This is a noble and praiseworthy trait in Islam. In questions of faith, however, we must acknowledge that there is a tendency among some Muslims to view themselves as "true believers" and to regard non-Muslims disdainfully as unbelievers or infidels. The world of the fundamentalist is divided into two territories, *Dar al-Islam* (House of Islam) and *Dar al-Harb* (House of War). America, seen by many as the leader of the Free World, is seen by Muslim fundamentalists as the leader of the House of War.

In the fundamentalist view, the will of God mandates that true believers hold the reigns of power in society. This insures that the law of God is maintained, and provides unbelievers with an opportunity and impetus to embrace Islam. The mindset that other faiths are either incomplete or false, makes it difficult for fundamentalist Muslims to accept that infidels or unbelievers can rule over Muslims. Many fundamentalist Muslims believe this violates God's natural order, corrupts the law of God, and weakens the "True Faith". Thus, whenever there is a large Muslim population in a non-Islamic country, there is an almost involuntary urge to invoke jihad to gain independence from the infidel. Those who stand in the way of this dream are "enemies of God." To this extremist group, the most contemptible of murderers who wraps himself in the banner of Islam is embraced as a brother, or even a hero, as long as he fights the "enemies of God." Yet, from the *Hadith* we know very well whom Muhammad considered the greatest enemy of Islam:

> The greatest enemies of God are those who are entered into Islam, and do acts of infidelity, and who, without cause, shed the blood of man.

Winning Hearts and Minds

If a Muslim truly wants to help mankind embrace the religion of God, then he must embody the virtues and spirituality which is at the heart of Islam. His life must be a living prayer, a tribute to the perfect example of living faith which Muhammad demonstrated, an example which unfortunately is not widely recognised in the West. Muhammad was accessible and charitable to all, a well of kindness from which all could draw. It is known that the lowliest of servants who felt abused by his master, would take Muhammad's hand and pull Him to his master to gain release or proper treatment. He taught that if a person offers you peace, you should not say, "but you aren't a believer." He was stern with criminals, but forgiving to those who wronged Him personally. He forgave and pardoned Habrar who was responsible for the death of His pregnant daughter, when he intentionally knocked her from her horse with his lance. He was tolerant and warned Muslims that whoever wrongs a Jew or a Christian, would have Him as his accuser. He taught that kindness is the mark of faith and whoever lacks this quality lacks faith. He taught that if you love God, you love your fellow human beings. He taught that all creatures are God's family, and the most beloved among them is the one who does the most good for all. He taught that malice and hatred destroy heavenly rewards. He taught that envy consumes the soul. He taught that we, male and female, should seek knowledge from cradle to grave, and go to the ends of the earth to acquire it. He taught that there is nothing more beautiful or perfect than Reason.

As previously mentioned, terrorism is the direct result of fanaticism, bigotry, hatred and rage, which flourish in an atmosphere of poverty, ignorance, injustice, oppression, and frustration. In the West, some well-meaning commentators see the rise of extremism and terrorism in Islamic societies as a reaction to poverty. Again, Muhammad's life is an example for Muslims. Muhammad proudly said, "Poverty is My glory." He swept His own floor, patched His own shoes and garments, milked goats, and kindled His own fire. He ate sitting on the floor, slept on a palm-fibre cot, sat on leather mats, drank from leather waterbags, and lived in a modest mud brick house. He said, "I am a servant, I eat and sleep like a servant."[85] Regretfully, the screaming faces of enraged extremists frame the image which many in the West have of Islam. Muhammad, however, was mild, soft-spoken, thoughtful, conciliatory and reasonable. In the *Qur'án* He revealed, "and verily whoso is patient and forgiveth -lo! That, verily, is of the steadfast heart of things."[86] " 'O my son! be steadfast in prayer, and bid what is reasonable and forbid what is wrong; be patient of what befalls thee, verily, that is one of the determined affairs. And twist not thy cheek proudly, nor walk in the land haughtily; verily, God loves not every arrogant boaster: but be moderate in thy walk, and lower thy voice; verily, the most disagreeable of voices is the voice of asses!' "[87]

The extremists and terrorists who cover His example and message with the blood of the innocent, do harm to the cause of Islam, but fair-minded people understand that the isolated acts of crazed individuals do not represent an entire religion. We do not associate Judaism with Baruch Goldstein, who murdered scores of unarmed Muslims in a Mosque in Hebron. Nor do we associate Christianity with white-supremacists, or I.R.A. terrorists. No, one must not form an opinion of a religion, based upon isolated acts of misguided individuals. "The objective observer notes that Jews were appalled by the actions of Baruch Goldstein and his murderous act was openly and unequivocally deplored by Jews worldwide." This allowed the world to see that this was an act of an isolated individual.

The greatest harm is done to Islam when Muslims fail to unreservedly censure such acts and to distance themselves from those who perpetrate them. If we can believe public opinion polls, two months after the attacks on the Twin Towers, eleven per cent of Muslims in Britain considered the attacks, "a good thing". Even if the poll were not truly representative because those questioned were leaving a mosque, that is still shocking, perhaps even more shocking. Those who call upon Americans and Jews to be killed wherever they are found, are considered by significant numbers of Muslims as, "strugglers in the path of God." They are celebrated on "the street" and on Al Jazeera television as heroes and defenders of Islam. Condemnation of their acts by prominent Muslims, was often reticent, restrained, and conditioned by a "but". The Islamic press has shocked many in the West. A Pakistani newspaper, *The Nation*, printed this editorial reaction: "September 11 was not mindless terrorism for terrorism's sake. It was reaction and revenge, even retribution."

It is worth noting that the people of Pakistan do not owe their independence to jihad, they owe their independence in great measure to Gandhi, an astute Hindu leader whose weapons were spirituality and political savvy. He employed non-violent civil disobedience, or "truth and firmness" as he called it, to win independence for the subcontinent. He fasted to end disturbances between Hindus and Muslims, and again to improve the status of the lower castes. He embodied the virtues taught by Christ and eventually shamed Christians into practising what they preached. Gandhi won the hearts and minds of the world because he followed the guidance of the Compassionate and Merciful God. Even after Mohammed Ali Jinnah championed the creation of Pakistan, he still proposed a unified foreign policy and defence strategy for India and Pakistan. Although he foresaw Pakistan as a Islamic state, it was to be a pluralistic and religiously tolerant nation. His hope was that Hindus would remain as citizens of Pakistan. Indeed he was a symbol of Hindu and Muslim unity when he had joined the Indian nationalist movement as a young man.

Contrast Gandhi and Jinnah with the image presented to the world of a Muslim cleric of the Wahhabi sect who praised and thanked Bin Laden for the death and destruction of the

World Trade Center attacks. The Shaykh gleefully recounted to Bin Laden his reaction (and that of other Saudi clerics) to the attacks:

> ...all of a sudden the news came and everyone was overjoyed and everyone, until the next day, in the morning, was talking about what was happening and we stayed until four o'clock, listening to the news, every time a little bit different, everyone was very joyous and saying "Allah is great," "Allah is great," "We are thankful to Allah," "Praise Allah." And I was happy for the happiness of my brothers. That day the congratulations were coming on the phone non-stop. The mother was receiving phone calls continuously. Thank Allah. Allah is great, praise be to Allah.

Abu Guaith, one of Bin Laden's lieutenants, described with satisfaction the reaction of Muslims which was broadcast on an Arab television station:

> The TV broadcasted the big event. The scene was showing an Egyptian family sitting in their living room, they exploded with joy. Do you know when there is a soccer game and your team wins? It was the same expression of joy. There was a subtitle that read: " 'In revenge for the children of Al Aqsa', Osama Bin Ladin executes an operation against America."

It may be that a few social misfits and malcontents subsequently expressed an interest in Islam, but imagine the harm done to the perception of Islam in the eyes of ordinary people. The sympathetic reaction of large numbers of Muslims to militant fanatical extremists, and their retreat to ultra-conservative fundamentalism does not win the hearts and minds of members of other faiths. It merely identifies the banner of Islam with hatred, bigotry, violence and fanaticism. Is this to be Muhammad's legacy?

'Abdu'l-Bahá, in the book by cited previously, cautioned Muslims with these words:

> One of the principal reasons why people of other religions have shunned and failed to become converted to the Faith of God is fanaticism and unreasoning religious zeal. See for example the divine words that were addressed to Muhammad, the Ark of Salvation, the Luminous Countenance and Lord of Men, bidding Him to be gentle with the people and long-suffering: "Debate with them in the kindliest manner."[88] That Blessed Tree Whose light was "neither of the East nor of the West"[89] and Who cast over all the peoples of the earth the sheltering shade of a measureless grace, showed forth infinite kindness and forbearance in His dealings with every one. In these words, likewise, were Moses and Aaron commanded to challenge Pharaoh, Lord of the Stakes:[90] "Speak ye to him with gentle speech."[91]

> Although the noble conduct of the Prophets and Holy Ones of God is widely known, and it is indeed... an excellent pattern for all mankind to follow, nevertheless some have remained neglectful of and separated from these qualities of extraordinary sympathy and loving-kindness, and have been prevented from attaining to the inner significances of the Holy Books. Not only do they scrupulously shun the adherents of religions other than their own, they do not even permit themselves to show them common courtesy. If one is not allowed to associate with another, how can one guide him out of the dark and empty night of denial, of "there-is-no-God," into the bright morning of belief, and the affirmation, "but God."[92] ... If a true believer when meeting an individual from a foreign country should express revulsion, and should speak the horrible words forbidding association with foreigners and referring to them as "unclean," the stranger would be grieved and

offended to such a point that he would never accept the Faith, even if he should see, taking place before his very eyes, the miracle of the splitting of the moon. The results of shunning him would be this, that if there had been in his heart some faint inclination toward God, he would repent of it, and would flee away from the sea of faith into the wastes of oblivion and unbelief. And upon returning home to his own country he would publish in the press statements to the effect that such and such a nation was utterly lacking in the qualifications of a civilized people.

If we ponder a while over the *Qur'ánic* verses and proofs, and the traditional accounts which have come down to us from those stars of the heaven of Divine Unity, the Holy Imáms, we shall be convinced of the fact that if a soul is endowed with the attributes of true faith and characterized with spiritual qualities he will become to all mankind an emblem of the outstretched mercies of God. For the attributes of the people of faith are justice and fair-mindedness; forbearance and compassion and generosity; consideration for others; candor, trustworthiness, and loyalty; love and loving-kindness; devotion and determination and humanity. If therefore an individual is truly righteous, he will avail himself of all those means which will attract the hearts of men, and through the attributes of God he will draw them to the straight path of faith and cause them to drink from the river of everlasting life.

Today we have closed our eyes to every righteous act and have sacrificed the abiding happiness of society to our own transitory profit. We regard fanaticism and zealotry as redounding to our credit and honor, and not content with this, we denounce one another and plot each other's ruin, and whenever we wish to put on a show of wisdom and learning, of virtue and godliness, we set about mocking and reviling this one and that. "The ideas of such a one," we say, "are wide of the mark, and so-and-so's behavior leaves much to be desired. The religious observances of Zayd are few and far between, and 'Amr is not firm in his faith. So-and-so's opinions smack of Europe... What is this heathenish religion, this idolatrous kind of error! Alas for the Law, alas for the Faith, alas for all these calamities! O Brothers in the Faith! This is surely the end of the world! The Judgment is coming!"

With words such as these they assault the minds of the helpless masses and disturb the hearts of the already bewildered poor, who know nothing of the true state of affairs and the real basis for all such talk, and remain completely unaware of the fact that a thousand selfish purposes are concealed behind the supposedly religious eloquence of certain individuals. They imagine that speakers of this type are motivated by virtuous zeal, when the truth is that such individuals keep up a great hue and cry because they see their own personal ruin in the welfare of the masses, and believe that if the people's eyes are opened, their own light will go out. Only the keenest insight will detect the fact that if the hearts of these individuals were really impelled by righteousness and the fear of God, the fragrance of it would, like musk, be spreading everywhere. Nothing in the world can ever be supported by words alone.

The spiritually learned, those who have derived infinite significance and wisdom from the *Book of Divine Revelation*, and whose illumined hearts draw inspiration from the unseen world of God, certainly exert their efforts to bring about the supremacy of the true followers of God, in all respects and above all peoples, and they toil and struggle to make use of every agency that will conduce to progress. If any man neglects these high purposes he can never prove acceptable in the sight of God; he stands out with all his shortcomings and claims perfection, and destitute, pretends to wealth.

Knowledge, purity, devotion, discipline, independence, have nothing to do with outer appearance and dress... A good character is in the sight of God and His chosen ones and the possessors of insight, the most excellent and praiseworthy of all things, but always on condition that its center of emanation should be reason and knowledge and its base should be true moderation...[93]

'Abdu'l-Bahá

19
Islam and the Bahá'í Faith

And were the trees that are in the earth pens, and the sea ink with seven more seas to swell its tide, the words of God would not be spent; verily, God is mighty, wise![94]

From the Qur'án

Immerse yourselves in the ocean of My words, that ye may unravel its secrets, and discover all the pearls of wisdom that lie hid in its depths... This is the changeless Faith of God, eternal in the past, eternal in the future. Let him that seeketh, attain it; and as to him that hath refused to seek it—verily, God is Self-Sufficient, above any need of His creatures.[95]

Bahá'u'lláh

Many Muslims hold that the revelation of the word of God ended in the seventh century with the *Qur'án*. The Law is found in the *Qur'án* and in the Sunna (example) of Muhammad. As Islam began to spread outside Arabia, *ijtihad* (responsible individual opinion) was employed to cover topics not expressly covered in the *Qur'án* or Sunna. It requires the use of analogical reasoning and today moderate currents in Islam would like to see "responsible individual opinion" used more frequently to allow Islam to adapt to a modern world. However, this original thinking is considered dangerous by those in power and its use has been severely restricted. The final source of Law is *ijma* (consensus of the community) concerning the adoption of new opinions and the rejection of existing opinions. This is a gradual process which conservative fundamentalists aided by militant extremists frequently seek to limit through intimidation.

Obviously the automobile did not exist in the seventh century, but we know that the women of Muhammad's family rode horses, donkeys and camels—the primary sources of transportation available then. Thus one would imagine that "responsible individual opinion" would allow women to drive automobiles, motorcycles, and airplanes—the modes of transportation available today. One would be wrong in Saudi Arabia, not only are women prohibited from driving, they are not even permitted to sit in the front seat. The world was shocked to learn of the beating of women under the Taliban for making a sound when they walked, or for laughing. This brings to mind a passage from the *Qur'án* directed then at a group of Christians, "because of their breach of their Covenant, We cursed them and made their hearts grow hard; they change the Words from their (right) places and forget all good part of the Message that was sent them."[96] Measures taken to protect women in the seventh century from crude barbarians so that "they should not be annoyed" are used in the twenty-first century to oppress women. How, other than a fresh revelation from God, will Islam be able to adapt to a modern world? For that reason it is recorded in the *Qur'án*, "For each period is a Book revealed."[97]

Many Muslims believe the *Qur'án* will only be modified and expanded once Qíyámah (The Day of Judgement) has occurred. Muhammad claimed to be a mortal man with a Divine revelation. He revealed, "But there never came an apostle to them but they mocked at him." Indeed, He was mocked and called upon to produce a miracle, to which He replied that the *Qur'án* was His miracle. How strange that His followers would follow those who denied Muhammad by expecting a supernatural spectacle on the Day of Judgement. Bahá'u'lláh taught that the Day of Judgement occurs every time a Prophet reveals a message from God. Those who recognise and accept the truth are born again. The Founders of the great religions such as Zoroaster, Abraham, Moses, Krishna, Buddha, Jesus, Muhammad, the Báb, and Bahá'u'lláh are Manifestations of God on earth. They represent a perfect reflection of God's light and virtue in human frame. Those who were physically present when the Manifestations of God walked among men, "attained unto the Divine Presence" if they saw with the eye of the spirit. Those who expect to see a supernatural event will remain blind to the truth, as did those who rejected Muhammad and the Prophets of old. For clearly no ordinary being can expect to see God since, "No vision taketh in Him, but He taketh in all vision."[98]

The Bahá'í Faith fulfils the heartfelt wish of many sincere Muslims to adapt Islam to the modern world. This could not have been achieved through human agencies, however well-meaning, for in the *Qur'án* it is recorded, "None of Our revelations do We abrogate or cause to be forgotten but We substitute something better or similar."[99] Bahá'u'lláh's revelation should be weighed against that standard.[100]

His revelation abolishes the concept of jihad, removes the notion that people of other faiths are "inferior" or "unclean", removes restrictions on women and declares them equal, calls for compulsory education for boys and girls, declares the unity of faith and reason, proclaims the harmony of science and religion, allows people to choose their own clothing and cut of beard, summons the adoption of a world court to settle disputes between and among nations, calls for an assembly of nations, recommends the adoption of a universal auxiliary language to be taught in schools worldwide, approves of democracy, warns of materialism, allows interest to be charged, rejects superstition, warns of the dangers of fanaticism, and calls for the establishment of the Most Great Peace.

His revelation also abrogates communal obligatory daily prayers. He revealed three obligatory daily prayers, any of which the individual is free to recite. This is done in private communion with God. He shunned elaborate rituals and ceremonials. In Houses of Worship (Mashriqu'l-Adhkár) there is no pulpit, altar, sermon or expounding of the law. The only words spoken, chanted or sung are prayers and passages from the scriptures of the religions of the world. Thus there are no priests, rabbis, or mullahs. He also expanded the concept of the "people of the book" explaining:

> There can be no doubt whatever that the peoples of the world, of whatever race or religion, derive their inspiration from one heavenly Source, and are the subjects of one God. The differences between the ordinances under which they abide should be attributed to the varying requirements and exigencies of the age in which they were revealed. All of them, except a few which are the outcome of human perversity, were ordained of God, and are a reflection of His Will and Purpose.[101]

Thus readings in a House of Worship might typically include prayers and passages from the *Bahá'í Writings*, the *Qur'án*, the *Bible*, the *Bhagavad-Gita*, or the teaching of Buddha.

In order to allow the Faith to adapt to an ever changing world, Bahá'u'lláh called for the establishment of a Universal House of Justice to rule upon matters not found in the Bahá'í writings. The Universal House of Justice, currently made up of nine male members, is democratically elected every five years when Bahá'í representatives from around the world, male and female, gather for this purpose. Matters found in the sacred writings may not be changed, but future members of the Universal Houses of Justices can, when necessary, abrogate or modify previous rulings of that body.

Bahá'u'lláh designated His son, 'Abdu'l-Bahá, as the Exemplar of His teachings, and the authorised interpreter of His teachings. In his will and testament, 'Abdu'l-Bahá extended the right to interpret the teachings to Shoghi Effendi, his grandson. Shoghi Effendi did not name a successor for this purpose, however, in 1963, six years after his passing, the first Universal House of Justice was elected. Since the question of expanding and interpreting the Law was specified by Bahá'u'lláh, there is no need for *qadis* (judges), *muftis* (exponents of the law), *mujtahids* or *mullahs* (expounders of the law).

Islam is upheld by five pillars: the declaration that there is one God and Muhammad is His Prophet, prayer, almsgiving, fasting, and pilgrimage. Some claim erroneously that jihad is the sixth pillar. Muhammad declared that making peace is more important than three of the pillars: prayer, almsgiving, and fasting. Thus it would seem that the best way to serve God is to make peace and to help others to recognise God and accept Muhammad as His Prophet.

Notwithstanding Bahá'u'lláh's imprisonment and the persecution of Bahá'ís in Islamic countries, within a hundred years of His ascension millions of Hindus, Christians, Buddhists, Jews, Zoroastrians, Jains and others have become Bahá'ís. All of them worship one God and accept Muhammad as His Prophet. As someone who has defended Muhammad and the *Qur'án* among Christians in the West, I will, as the *Qur'án* states, tell you the truth even when it hurts. The widespread extremism and militancy in the name of Islam has overshadowed the beauty of Muhammad and His revelation in the eyes of many, as has the backwardness, bigotry and intolerance in many Islamic countries. Christ taught His followers to judge a Prophet by His fruits. When hostages are beheaded in the name of God, when jets are rammed into buildings to the cries of "God is Great", or when suicidal commandos attack the Indian parliament, then it is no surprise when a Christian leader like Franklin Graham proclaims, "I don't believe this is a wonderful, peaceful religion."

Moreover, the vast majority of those who enjoy liberty, democracy, a free press, free expression, freedom of movement, and religious freedom are unlikely to submit to Islamic law (Shariah). What then is the alternative? Those who dream of jihad have created a nightmare, and the war they seek could result in the destruction of mankind. I ask you to sincerely investigate the revelation of Bahá'u'lláh and to judge fairly if there is a better way to spread belief in God and peace on earth.

> O peoples of the earth! Haste ye to do the pleasure of God, and war ye valiantly, as it behooveth you to war, for the sake of proclaiming His resistless and immovable Cause. We have decreed that war shall be waged in the path of God with the armies of wisdom and utterance, and of a goodly character and praiseworthy deeds...Beware lest ye shed the blood of any one. Unsheathe the sword of your tongue from the scabbard of utterance, for therewith ye can conquer the citadels of men's hearts. We have abolished the law to wage holy war against each other. God's mercy hath, verily, encompassed all created things, if ye do but understand.[102]
>
> *Bahá'u'lláh*

Every age hath its own problem, and every soul its particular aspiration. The remedy the world needeth in its present-day afflictions can never be the same as that which a subsequent age may require. Be anxiously concerned with the needs of the age ye live in, and center your deliberations on its exigencies and requirements.

We can well perceive how the whole human race is encompassed with great, with incalculable afflictions. We see it languishing on its bed of sickness, sore-tried and disillusioned. They that are intoxicated by self-conceit have interposed themselves between it and the Divine and infallible Physician. Witness how they have entangled all men, themselves included, in the mesh of their devices. They can neither discover the cause of the disease, nor have they any knowledge of the remedy. They have conceived the straight to be crooked, and have imagined their friend an enemy.

Incline your ears to the sweet melody of this Prisoner. Arise, and lift up your voices, that haply they that are fast asleep may be awakened.[103]

Bahá'u'lláh

20
Passages from the
Revelation of Bahá'u'lláh

O ye that dwell on earth! The distinguishing feature that marketh the pre-eminent character of this Supreme Revelation consisteth in that We have, on the one hand, blotted out from the pages of God's holy Book whatsoever hath been the cause of strife, of malice and mischief amongst the children of men, and have, on the other, laid down the essential prerequisites of concord, of understanding, of complete and enduring unity. Well is it with them that keep My statutes.

Time and again have We admonished Our beloved ones to avoid, nay to flee from, anything whatsoever from which the odour of mischief can be detected. The world is in great turmoil, and the minds of its people are in a state of utter confusion. We entreat the Almighty that He may graciously illuminate them with the glory of His Justice, and enable them to discover that which will be profitable unto them at all times and under all conditions. He, verily is the All-Possessing, the Most High.

That the divers communions of the earth, and the manifold systems of religious belief, should never be allowed to foster the feelings of animosity among men, is, in this Day, of the essence of the Faith of God and His Religion. These principles and laws, these firmly-established and mighty systems, have proceeded from one Source, and are rays of one Light. That they differ one from another is to be attributed to the varying requirements of the ages in which they were promulgated.

Gird up the loins of your endeavor, O people of Bahá, that haply the tumult of religious dissension and strife that agitateth the peoples of the earth may be stilled, that every trace of it may be completely obliterated. For the love of God, and them that serve Him, arise to aid this sublime and momentous Revelation...

The utterance of God is a lamp, whose light is these words: Ye are the fruits of one tree, and the leaves of one branch. Deal ye one with another with the utmost love and harmony, with friendliness and fellowship. He Who is the Daystar of Truth beareth Me witness! So powerful is the light of unity that it can illuminate the whole earth. The One true God, He Who knoweth all things, Himself testifieth to the truth of these words.

O ye children of men! The fundamental purpose animating the Faith of God and His Religion is to safeguard the interests and promote the unity of the human race, and to foster the spirit of love and fellowship amongst men, suffer it not to become a source of dissension and discord, of hate and enmity. This is the straight Path, the fixed and immovable foundation. Whatsoever is raised on this foundation, the changes and chances of the world can never impair its strength, nor will the revolution of countless centuries undermine its structure. Our hope is that the world's religious leaders and the rulers thereof will unitedly arise for the reformation of this age and the rehabilitation of its fortunes. Let them, after meditating on its needs, take counsel together and, through anxious and full deliberation, administer to a diseased and sorely-afflicted world the remedy it requireth....

O people of the earth! The first Glad-Tidings... in this Most Great Revelation, imparted unto all the peoples of the world is that the law of holy war hath been blotted out from the Book. Glorified be the All-Merciful, the Lord of grace abounding, through Whom the door of heavenly bounty hath been flung open in the face of all that are in heaven and on earth.

It is permitted that the peoples and kindreds of the world associate with one another with joy and radiance. O people! Consort with the followers of all religions in a spirit of friendliness and fellowship. Thus hath the daystar of His sanction and authority shone forth above the horizon of the decree of God, the Lord of the worlds.

It behoveth the sovereigns of the world—may God assist them—or the ministers of the earth to take counsel together and to adopt one of the existing languages or a new one to be taught to children in schools throughout the world, and likewise one script. Thus the whole earth will come to be regarded as one country.

It is binding and incumbent upon the peoples of the world, one and all, to extend aid unto this momentous Cause which is come from the heaven of the Will of the ever-abiding God, that perchance the fire of animosity which blazeth in the hearts of some of the peoples of the earth may, through the living waters of divine wisdom and by virtue of heavenly counsels and exhortations, be quenched, and the light of unity and concord may shine forth and shed its radiance upon the world.

We cherish the hope that through the earnest endeavours of such as are the exponents of the power of God—exalted be His glory—the weapons of war throughout the world may be converted into instruments of reconstruction and that strife and conflict may be removed from the midst of men.

Were anyone to ponder in his heart that which hath, in this Revelation, streamed forth from the Pen of Glory, he would be assured that whatever this Wronged One hath affirmed He hath had no intention of establishing any position or distinction for Himself. The purpose hath rather been to attract the souls, through the sublimity of His words, unto the summit of transcendent glory and to endow them with the capacity of perceiving that which will purge and purify the peoples of the world from the strife and dissension which religious differences provoke. Unto this bear witness My heart, My Pen, My inner and My outer Being. God grant that all men may turn unto the treasuries latent within their own beings.

O ye rich ones on earth! The poor in your midst are My trust; guard ye My trust, and be not intent only on your own ease.

If ye meet the abased or the down-trodden, turn not away disdainfully from them, for the King of Glory ever watcheth over them and surroundeth them with such tenderness as none can fathom except them that have suffered their wishes and desires to be merged in the Will of your Lord, the Gracious, the All-Wise. O ye rich ones of the earth! Flee not from the face of the poor that lieth in the dust, nay rather befriend him and suffer him to recount the tale of the woes with which God's inscrutable Decree hath caused him to be afflicted... Blessed are the learned that pride not themselves on their attainments; and well is it with the righteous that mock not the sinful, but rather conceal their misdeeds, so that their own shortcomings may remain veiled to men's eyes.

The pious deeds of the monks and priests among the followers of the Spirit [Jesus]—upon Him be the peace of God— are remembered in His presence. In this Day, however, let them give up the life of seclusion and direct their steps towards the open world and busy themselves with that which will profit themselves and others. We have granted them leave to enter into wedlock that they may bring forth one who will make mention of God, the Lord of the seen and the unseen, the Lord of the Exalted Throne.

When the sinner findeth himself wholly detached and freed from all save God, he should beg forgiveness and pardon from

Him. Confession of sins and transgressions before human beings is not permissible, as it hath never been nor will ever be conducive to divine forgiveness. Moreover such confession before people results in one's humiliation and abasement, and God—exalted be His glory—wisheth not the humiliation of His servants. Verily He is the Compassionate, the Merciful.

O people of Bahá! Ye are the dawning-places of the love of God and the daysprings of His loving-kindness. Defile not your tongues with the cursing and reviling of any soul, and guard your eyes against that which is not seemly. Set forth that which ye possess. If it be favourably received, your end is attained; if not, to protest is vain. Leave that soul to himself and turn unto the Lord, the Protector, the Self-Subsisting. Be not the cause of grief, much less of discord and strife. The hope is cherished that ye may obtain true education in the shelter of the tree of His tender mercies and act in accordance with that which God desireth. Ye are all the leaves of one tree and the drops of one ocean.

They that are endued with sincerity and faithfulness should associate with all the peoples and kindreds of the earth with joy and radiance, inasmuch as consorting with people hath promoted and will continue to promote unity and concord, which in turn are conducive to the maintenance of order in the world and to the regeneration of nations. Blessed are such as hold fast to the cord of kindliness and tender mercy and are free from animosity and hatred.

O contending peoples and kindreds of the earth! Set your faces towards unity, and let the radiance of its light shine upon you. Gather ye together, and for the sake of God resolve to root out whatever is the source of contention amongst you. Then will the effulgence of the world's great Luminary envelop the whole earth, and its inhabitants become the citizens of one city, and the occupants of one and the same throne. This wronged

One hath, ever since the early days of His life, cherished none other desire but this, and will continue to entertain no wish except this wish. There can be no doubt whatever that the peoples of the world, of whatever race or religion, derive their inspiration from one heavenly Source, and are the subjects of one God. The difference between the ordinances under which they abide should be attributed to the varying requirements and exigencies of the age in which they were revealed. All of them, except a few which are the outcome of human perversity, were ordained of God, and are a reflection of His Will and Purpose. Arise and, armed with the power of faith, shatter to pieces the gods of your vain imaginings, the sowers of dissension amongst you. Cleave unto that which draweth you together and uniteth you.

Justice is, in this day, bewailing its plight, and Equity groaneth beneath the yoke of oppression. The thick clouds of tyranny have darkened the face of the earth, and enveloped its peoples. Through the movement of Our Pen of glory We have, at the bidding of the omnipotent Ordainer, breathed a new life into every human frame, and instilled into every word a fresh potency. All created things proclaim the evidences of this worldwide regeneration. This is the most great, the most joyful tidings imparted by the Pen of this wronged One to mankind...

O people of God! Do not busy yourselves in your own concerns; let your thoughts be fixed upon that which will rehabilitate the fortunes of mankind and sanctify the hearts and souls of men. This can best be achieved through pure and holy deeds, through a virtuous life and a goodly behavior. Valiant acts will ensure the triumph of this Cause, and a saintly character will reinforce its power. Cleave unto righteousness, O people of Baha! This, verily, is the commandment which this wronged One hath given unto you, and the first choice of His unrestrained Will for everyone of you.

It is incumbent upon every man, in this Day, to hold fast unto whatsoever will promote the interests, and exalt the station, of all nations and just governments. Through each and every one of the verses which the Pen of the Most High hath revealed, the doors of love and unity have been unlocked and flung open to the face of men... Whatsoever hath led the children of men to shun one another, and hath caused dissensions and divisions amongst them, hath, through the revelation of these words, been nullified and abolished. From the heaven of God's Will, and for the purpose of ennobling the world of being and of elevating the minds and souls of men, hath been sent down that which is the most effective instrument for the education of the whole human race. The highest essence and most perfect expression of whatsoever the peoples of old have either said or written hath, through this most potent Revelation, been sent down from the heaven of the Will of the All-Possessing, the Ever-Abiding God. Of old it hath been revealed: "Love of one's country is an element of the Faith of God."

The Tongue of Grandeur hath, however, in the day of His manifestation proclaimed: "It is not his to boast who loveth his country, but it is his who loveth the world." Through the power released by these exalted words He hath lent a fresh impulse, and set a new direction, to the birds of men's hearts, and hath obliterated every trace of restriction and limitation from God's holy Book.

O people of Justice! Be as brilliant as the light, and as splendid as the fire that blazed in the Burning Bush. The brightness of the fire of your love will no doubt fuse and unify the contending peoples and kindreds of the earth, whilst the fierceness of the flame of enmity and hatred cannot but result in strife and ruin...

The summons and the message which We gave were never intended to reach or to benefit one land or one people only. Mankind in its entirety must firmly adhere to whatsoever hath been revealed and vouchsafed unto it. Then and only then will it attain unto true liberty. The whole earth is illuminated with the resplendent glory of God's Revelation... Behold how the generality of mankind hath been endued with the capacity to hearken unto God's most exalted Word—the Word upon which must depend the gathering together and spiritual resurrection of all men....

Incline your hearts, O people of God, unto the counsels of your true, your incomparable Friend. The Word of God may be likened unto a sapling, whose roots have been implanted in the hearts of men. It is incumbent upon you to foster its growth through the living waters of wisdom, of sanctified and holy words, so that its root may become firmly fixed and its branches may spread out as high as the heavens and beyond.

The world is in great turmoil, and the minds of its people are in a state of utter confusion. We entreat the Almighty that He may graciously illuminate them with the glory of His Justice, and enable them to discover that which will be profitable unto them at all times and under all conditions. He, verily is the All-Possessing, the Most High.

The One true God beareth Me witness, and His creatures will testify, that not for a moment did I allow Myself to be hidden from the eyes of men, nor did I consent to shield My person from their injury. Before the face of all men I have arisen, and bidden them fulfil My pleasure. My object is none other than the betterment of the world and the tranquillity of its peoples. The well-being of mankind, its peace and security, are unattainable unless and until its unity is firmly established. This unity can never be achieved so long as the counsels which the Pen of the Most High hath revealed are suffered to pass unheeded.

Through the power of the words He hath uttered the whole of the human race can be illumined with the light of unity, and the remembrance of His Name is able to set on fire the hearts of all men, and burn away the veils that intervene between them and His glory. One righteous act is endowed with a potency that can so elevate the dust as to cause it to pass beyond the heaven of heavens. It can tear every bond asunder, and hath the power to restore the force that hath spent itself and vanished....

Be pure, O people of God, be pure; be righteous, be righteous.... Say: O people of God! That which can ensure the victory of Him Who is the Eternal Truth, His hosts and helpers on earth, have been set down in the sacred Books and Scriptures, and are as clear and manifest as the sun. These hosts are such righteous deeds, such conduct and character, as are acceptable in His sight. Whoso ariseth, in this Day, to aid Our Cause, and summoneth to his assistance the hosts of a praiseworthy character and upright conduct, the influence flowing from such an action will, most certainly, be diffused throughout the whole world.

More grievous became Our plight from day to day, nay, from hour to hour, until they took Us forth from Our prison and made Us, with glaring injustice, enter the Most Great Prison. And if anyone ask them: 'For what crime were they imprisoned?' they would answer and say: 'They, verily, sought to supplant the Faith with a new religion!' If that which is ancient be what ye prefer, wherefore, then, have ye discarded that which hath been set down in the *Torah* and the Evangel? Clear it up, O men! By My life! There is no place for you to flee to in this day. If this be My crime, then Muhammad, the Apostle of God, committed it before Me, and before Him He Who was the Spirit of God (Jesus Christ), and yet earlier He Who conversed with God (Moses). And if My sin be this, that I have exalted the Word of God and revealed His Cause, then indeed am I the greatest of sinners! Such a sin I will not barter for the kingdoms of earth and heaven.

My imprisonment doeth Me no harm, neither the tribulations I suffer, nor the things that have befallen Me at the hands of My oppressors. That which harmeth Me is the conduct of those who, though they bear My name, yet commit that which maketh My heart and My pen to lament. They that spread disorder in the land, and lay hands on the property of others, and enter a house without leave of its owner, We, verily, are clear of them, unless they repent and return unto God, the Ever-Forgiving, the Most Merciful.

Beware lest ye shed the blood of any one. Unsheathe the sword of your tongue from the scabbard of utterance, for therewith ye can conquer the citadels of men's hearts. We have abolished the law to wage holy war against each other. God's mercy hath, verily, encompassed all created things, if ye do but understand.

O peoples of the earth! Haste ye to do the pleasure of God, and war ye valiantly, as it behooveth you to war, for the sake of proclaiming His resistless and immovable Cause. We have decreed that war shall be waged in the path of God with the armies of wisdom and utterance, and of a goodly character and praiseworthy deeds. Thus hath it been decided by Him Who is the All-Powerful, the Almighty. There is no glory for him that committeth disorder on the earth after it hath been made so good. Fear God, O people, and be not of them that act unjustly.

That one indeed is a man who, today, dedicateth himself to the service of the entire human race. The Great Being saith: Blessed and happy is he that ariseth to promote the best interests of the peoples and kindreds of the earth. In another passage He hath proclaimed: It is not for him to pride himself who loveth his own country, but rather for him who loveth the whole world. The earth is but one country, and mankind its citizens.

Such exhortations to union and concord as are inscribed in the *Books of the Prophets* by the Pen of the Most High bear reference unto specific matters; not a union that would lead to disunity or a concord which would create discord. This is the station where measures are set unto everything, a station where every deserving soul shall be given his due. Well is it with them that appreciate the meaning and grasp the intent of these words, and woe betide the heedless. Unto this all the evidences of nature, in their very essences, bear ample testimony. Every discerning man of wisdom is well acquainted with that which We have mentioned, but not those who have strayed far from the living fountain of fairmindedness and are roving distraught in the wilderness of ignorance and blind fanaticism.

O my friend! In all circumstances one should seize upon every means which will promote security and tranquillity among the peoples of the world. The Great Being saith: In this glorious Day whatever will purge you from corruption and will lead you towards peace and composure, is indeed the Straight Path.

Please God, the peoples of the world may be led, as the result of the high endeavours exerted by their rulers and the wise and learned amongst men, to recognize their best interests. How long will humanity persist in its waywardness? How long will injustice continue? How long is chaos and confusion to reign amongst men? How long will discord agitate the face of society?

This humble servant is filled with wonder, inasmuch as all men are endowed with the capacity to see and hear, yet we find them deprived of the privilege of using these faculties. This servant hath been prompted to pen these lines by virtue of the tender love he cherisheth for thee. The winds of despair are, alas, blowing from every direction, and the strife that divideth and afflicteth the human race is daily increasing. The signs of impending convulsions and chaos can now be discerned, inasmuch as the prevailing order appeareth to be lamentably defective. I beseech God, exalted be His glory, that He may graciously awaken the peoples of the earth, may grant that the end of their conduct may be profitable unto them, and aid them to accomplish that which beseemeth their station.

Were man to appreciate the greatness of his station and the loftiness of his destiny he would manifest naught save goodly character, pure deeds, and a seemly and praiseworthy conduct. If the learned and wise men of goodwill were to impart guidance unto the people, the whole earth would be regarded as one country. Verily this is the undoubted truth. This servant appealeth to every diligent and enterprising soul to exert his utmost endeavour and arise to rehabilitate the conditions in all regions and to quicken the dead with the living waters of wisdom and utterance, by virtue of the love he cherisheth for God, the One, the Peerless, the Almighty, the Beneficent.

Great is the station of man. Great must also be his endeavours for the rehabilitation of the world and the well-being of nations. I beseech the One true God to graciously confirm thee in that which beseemeth man's station.

Be generous in prosperity, and thankful in adversity. Be worthy of the trust of thy neighbor, and look upon him with a bright and friendly face. Be a treasure to the poor, an admonisher to the rich, an answerer of the cry of the needy, a preserver of the sanctity of thy pledge. Be fair in thy judgment, and guarded in thy speech. Be unjust to no man, and show all meekness to all men. Be as a lamp unto them that walk in darkness, a joy to the sorrowful, a sea for the thirsty, a haven for the distressed, an upholder and defender of the victim of oppression. Let integrity and uprightness distinguish all thine acts. Be a home for the stranger, a balm to the suffering, a tower of strength for the fugitive. Be eyes to the blind, and a guiding light unto the feet of the erring. Be an ornament to the countenance of truth, a crown to the brow of fidelity, a pillar of the temple of righteousness, a breath of life to the body of mankind, an ensign of the hosts of justice, a luminary above the horizon of virtue, a dew to the soil of the human heart, an ark on the ocean of knowledge, a sun in the heaven of bounty, a gem on the diadem of wisdom, a shining light in the firmament of thy generation, a fruit upon the tree of humility.

Every eye, in this Day, should seek what will best promote
the Cause of God. He, Who is the Eternal Truth, beareth Me
witness! Nothing whatever can, in this Day, inflict a greater harm
upon this Cause than dissension and strife, contention,
estrangement and apathy, among the loved ones of God. Flee
them, through the power of God and His sovereign aid, and
strive ye to knit together the hearts of men, in His Name, the
Unifier, the All-Knowing, the All-Wise.

Beseech ye the one true God to grant that ye may taste the
savor of such deeds as are performed in His path, and partake of
the sweetness of such humility and submissiveness as are shown
for His sake. Forget your own selves, and turn your eyes towards
your neighbor. Bend your energies to whatever may foster the
education of men. Nothing is, or can ever be, hidden from God.
If ye follow in His way, His incalculable and imperishable
blessings will be showered upon you.

Verily I say, such is the greatness of this Cause that the father
flieth from his son, and the son flieth from his father. Call ye to
mind the story of Noah and Canaan. God grant that, in these
days of heavenly delight, ye may not deprive yourselves of the
sweet savors of the All-Glorious God, and may partake, in this
spiritual Springtime, of the outpourings of His grace...

Who can ever believe that this Servant of God hath at any
time cherished in His heart a desire for any earthly honor or
benefit? The Cause associated with His Name is far above the
transitory things of this world. Behold Him, an exile, a victim
of tyranny, in this Most Great Prison. His enemies have assailed
Him on every side, and will continue to do so till the end of His
life. Whatever, therefore, He saith unto you is wholly for the
sake of God, that haply the peoples of the earth may cleanse
their hearts from the stain of evil desire, may rend its veil asunder,
and attain unto the knowledge of the one true God—the most
exalted station to which any man can aspire. Their belief or
disbelief in My Cause can neither profit nor harm Me. We

summon them wholly for the sake of God. He, verily, can afford
to dispense with all creatures.

O ye the elected representatives of the people in every land!
Take ye counsel together, and let your concern be only for that
which profiteth mankind, and bettereth the condition thereof,
if ye be of them that scan heedfully. Regard the world as the
human body which, though at its creation whole and perfect,
hath been afflicted, through various causes, with grave disorders
and maladies. Not for one day did it gain ease, nay its sickness
waxed more severe, as it fell under the treatment of ignorant
physicians, who gave full rein to their personal desires, and have
erred grievously. And if, at one time, through the care of an able
physician, a member of that body was healed, the rest remained
afflicted as before. Thus informeth you the All-Knowing, the
All-Wise.

We behold it, in this day, at the mercy of rulers so drunk
with pride that they cannot discern clearly their own best
advantage, much less recognize a Revelation so bewildering and
challenging as this. And whenever any one of them hath striven
to improve its condition, his motive hath been his own gain,
whether confessedly so or not; and the unworthiness of this
motive hath limited his power to heal or cure.

That which the Lord hath ordained as the sovereign remedy
and mightiest instrument for the healing of all the world is the
union of all its peoples in one universal Cause, one common
Faith. This can in no wise be achieved except through the power
of a skilled, an all-powerful and inspired Physician. This, verily,
is the truth, and all else naught but error.

To whatever place We may be banished, however great the
tribulation We may suffer, they who are the people of God must,
with fixed resolve and perfect confidence, keep their eyes directed
towards the Day Spring of Glory, and be busied in whatever
may be conducive to the betterment of the world and the
education of its peoples. All that hath befallen Us in the past

hath advanced the interests of Our Revelation and blazoned its fame; and all that may befall Us in the future will have a like result. Cling ye, with your inmost hearts, to the Cause of God, a Cause that hath been sent down by Him Who is the Ordainer, the All-Wise. We have, with the utmost kindliness and mercy, summoned and directed all peoples and nations to that which shall truly profit them.

The Daystar of Truth that shineth in its meridian splendor beareth Us witness! They who are the people of God have no ambition except to revive the world, to ennoble its life, and regenerate its peoples. Truthfulness and good-will have, at all times, marked their relations with all men. Their outward conduct is but a reflection of their inward life, and their inward life a mirror of their outward conduct. No veil hideth or obscureth the verities on which their Faith is established. Before the eyes of all men these verities have been laid bare, and can be unmistakably recognized. Their very acts attest the truth of these words.

Every discerning eye can, in this Day, perceive the dawning light of God's Revelation, and every attentive ear can recognize the Voice that was heard from the Burning Bush. Such is the rushing of the waters of Divine mercy, that He Who is the Day Spring of the signs of God and the Revealer of the evidences of His glory is without veil or concealment associating and conversing with the peoples of the earth and its kindreds. How numerous are those who, with hearts intent upon malice, have sought Our Presence, and departed from it loyal and loving friends! The portals of grace are wide open before the face of all men. In Our outward dealings with them We have treated alike the righteous and the sinner, that perchance the evil-doer may attain the limitless ocean of Divine forgiveness. Our name "the Concealer" hath shed such a light upon men that the froward hath imagined himself to be numbered with the pious. No man that seeketh Us will We ever disappoint, neither shall he that hath set his face towards Us be denied access unto Our court....

O friends! Help ye the one true God, exalted be His glory, by your goodly deeds, by such conduct and character as shall be acceptable in His sight. He that seeketh to be a helper of God in this Day, let him close his eyes to whatever he may possess, and open them to the things of God. Let him cease to occupy himself with that which profiteth him, and concern himself with that which shall exalt the all-compelling name of the Almighty...

O people! Sow not the seeds of discord among men, and refrain from contending with your neighbor, for your Lord hath committed the world and the cities thereof to the care of the kings of the earth... He hath refused to reserve for Himself any share whatever of this world's dominion. To this He Who is Himself the Eternal Truth will testify. The things He hath reserved for Himself are the cities of men's hearts, that He may cleanse them from all earthly defilements, and enable them to draw nigh unto the hallowed Spot... Open, O people, the city of the human heart with the key of your utterance. Thus have We, according to a pre-ordained measure, prescribed unto you your duty.

By the righteousness of God! The world and its vanities, and its glory, and whatever delights it can offer, are all, in the sight of God, as worthless as, nay, even more contemptible than, dust and ashes. Would that the hearts of men could comprehend it! Cleanse yourselves thoroughly, O people of Baha, from the defilement of the world, and of all that pertaineth unto it. God Himself beareth Me witness. The things of the earth ill beseem you. Cast them away unto such as may desire them, and fasten your eyes upon this most holy and effulgent Vision.

That which beseemeth you is the love of God, and the love of Him Who is the Manifestation of His Essence, and the observance of whatsoever He chooseth to prescribe unto you, did ye but know it. Say: Let truthfulness and courtesy be your adorning.

Suffer not yourselves to be deprived of the robe of forbearance and justice, that the sweet savors of holiness may be wafted from your hearts upon all created things. Say: Beware, O people of Baha, lest ye walk in the ways of them whose words differ from their deeds. Strive that ye may be enabled to manifest to the peoples of the earth the signs of God, and to mirror forth His commandments. Let your acts be a guide unto all mankind, for the professions of most men, be they high or low, differ from their conduct. It is through your deeds that ye can distinguish yourselves from others. Through them the brightness of your light can be shed upon the whole earth. Happy is the man that heedeth My counsel, and keepeth the precepts prescribed by Him Who is the All-Knowing, the All-Wise.

O Members of the human race! Hold ye fast by the Cord which no man can sever. This will, indeed, profit you all the days of your life, for its strength is of God, the Lord of all worlds. Cleave ye to justice and fairness, and turn away from the whisperings of the foolish...

Whoso cleaveth to justice, can, under no circumstances, transgress the limits of moderation. He discerneth the truth in all things, through the guidance of Him Who is the All-Seeing. The civilization, so often vaunted by the learned exponents of arts and sciences, will, if allowed to overleap the bounds of moderation, bring great evil upon men. Thus warneth you He Who is the All-Knowing. If carried to excess, civilization will prove as prolific a source of evil as it had been of goodness when kept within the restraints of moderation...

All other things are subject to this same principle of moderation... In this Day, We can neither approve the conduct of the fearful that seeketh to dissemble his faith, nor sanction the behavior of the avowed believer that clamorously asserteth his allegiance to this Cause. Both should observe the dictates of wisdom, and strive diligently to serve the best interests of the Faith.

When the victory arriveth, every man shall profess himself as believer and shall hasten to the shelter of God's Faith. Happy are they who in the days of world-encompassing trials have stood fast in the Cause and refused to swerve from its truth.

Appendix I

United Nations Resolution on the
Situation of the Bahá'í in Iran
Press Release from the Bahá'í World News Service

UNITED NATIONS, 19 December 2001 (BWNS)—For the 16th time in 17 years, the United Nations General Assembly has expressed "concern" over human rights violations in Iran, specifically noting the "still-existing discrimination" against the Bahá'i community of Iran.

By a vote of 72 to 49, with 46 abstentions, the Assembly passed a resolution on 19 December 2001 that calls on the Islamic Republic of Iran to "eliminate all forms of discrimination based on religious grounds" and, more specifically, asks the Iranian Government to fully implement previous United Nations recommendations that the Bahá'is be granted complete freedom to practice their religion.

The resolution followed a report issued in August by the UN Human Rights Commission's special representative on Iran, Professor Maurice Copithorne, that indicated that the 300,000-member Iranian Bahá'i community continues to experience discrimination in the areas of education, employment, travel, housing and the practice of religious activities.

More specifically, Prof. Copithorne said that Bahá'i property continues to be subject to confiscation. He indicated that a

number of Baha'i families were forced to leave their homes and
farmlands in the first months of 2001 in Kata, Buyr-Ahmand.
In 2000, he said, information was received that four buildings
were confiscated in Tehran, three in Shiraz and one in Isfahan.

"It is also reported that the issuance of business licenses to
Baha'is has been delayed and that some stores and business owned
by Baha'is have been closed," said Prof. Copithorne.

Prof. Copithorne also said that Baha'is continue to be denied
access to higher education in legally recognized public
institutions. "Recently three classrooms used by the Baha'is for
their own educational purposes were seized," he said.

"Baha'is are still, in effect, prevented from participation in
religious gatherings or educational activities," wrote Prof.
Copithorne.

In its resolution, the Assembly decided to continue
monitoring Iran next year, "paying particular attention to further
developments, including the situation of the Baha'is and other
minority groups."

Since the Islamic Revolutionary regime took power in Iran
in 1979, Baha'is have been harassed and persecuted solely on
account of their religious beliefs. More than 200 Baha'is have
been killed, hundreds have been imprisoned, and thousands have
been deprived of jobs, education or property. In 1983, all Baha'i
institutions were banned, and they remain officially closed.

Although the number of executions and imprisonments has
lessened in recent years, Baha'is in Iran remain without any
official recognition or legal protection that might protect them
from discrimination, said Bani Dugal, a Baha'i International
Community representative to the United Nations.

"We see these on-going actions—the imprisonment of
Baha'is, the confiscation of property, the deprivation of
education, the restrictions on travel and worship, and the
banning of Baha'i institutions—as evidence of the continuing

campaign of the government of Iran to strangle the Baha'i community of that country," said Ms. Dugal.

"The nature of the persecution is clearly based on religious belief," she continued. "Baha'is have repeatedly been offered relief from persecution if they were prepared to recant their Faith.

"So Baha'is continue to be viewed as 'unprotected infidels,' by the Government, without any form of legal protection, even though Iran is a signatory of the International Covenant on Civil and Political Rights which guarantees freedom of religious belief.

"The Baha'is seek no special privileges," Ms. Dugal said. "They desire only their rights under the International Bill of Human Rights, of which Iran is a signatory, including the right to life, the right to profess and practice their religion, the right to liberty and security of person, and the right to education and work."

UNO-BP-011219-1-IRANRESOLUTION-144-S

Appendix II

Dealing with
Murderers, Terrorists and Criminals

'Abdu'l-Bahá was asked: Should a criminal be punished,
or forgiven and his crime overlooked?

Answer.—There are two sorts of retributory punishments. One is vengeance, the other, chastisement. Man has not the right to take vengeance, but the community has the right to punish the criminal; and this punishment is intended to warn and to prevent so that no other person will dare to commit a like crime. This punishment is for the protection of man's rights, but it is not vengeance; vengeance appeases the anger of the heart by opposing one evil to another. This is not allowable, for man has not the right to take vengeance. But if criminals were entirely forgiven, the order of the world would be upset. So punishment is one of the essential necessities for the safety of communities, but he who is oppressed by a transgressor has not the right to take vengeance. On the contrary, he should forgive and pardon, for this is worthy of the world of man.

The communities must punish the oppressor, the murderer, the malefactor, so as to warn and restrain others from committing like crimes. But the most essential thing is that the people must be educated in such a way that no crimes will be committed; for it is possible to educate the masses so effectively that they will avoid and shrink from perpetrating crimes, so that the crime itself will appear to them as the greatest chastisement, the utmost condemnation and torment. Therefore, no crimes which require punishment will be committed.

We must speak of things that are possible of performance in this world. There are many theories and high ideas on this subject, but they are not practicable; consequently, we must speak of things that are feasible.

For example, if someone oppresses, injures and wrongs another, and the wronged man retaliates, this is vengeance and is censurable... The two actions are equivalent; if one action is reprehensible, both are reprehensible. The only difference is that one was committed first, the other later.

But the community has the right of defence and of self-protection; moreover, the community has no hatred nor animosity for the murderer: it imprisons or punishes him merely for the protection and security of others. It is not for the purpose of taking vengeance upon the murderer, but for the purpose of inflicting a punishment by which the community will be protected. If the community and the inheritors of the murdered one were to forgive and return good for evil, the cruel would be continually ill-treating others, and assassinations would continually occur. Vicious people, like wolves, would destroy the sheep of God. The community has no ill-will and rancour in the infliction of punishment, and it does not desire to appease the anger of the heart; its purpose is by punishment to protect others so that no atrocious actions may be committed.

Thus when Christ said: "Whosoever shall smite thee on the right cheek, turn to him the left one also"[Cf. Matt. 5:39], it was for the purpose of teaching men not to take personal revenge. He did not mean that, if a wolf should fall upon a flock of sheep and wish to destroy it, the wolf should be encouraged to do so. No, if Christ had known that a wolf had entered the fold and was about to destroy the sheep, most certainly He would have prevented it.

As forgiveness is one of the attributes of the Merciful One, so also justice is one of the attributes of the Lord. The tent of existence is upheld upon the pillar of justice and not upon forgiveness. The continuance of mankind depends upon justice and not upon forgiveness. So if, at present, the law of pardon were practised in all countries, in a short time the world would be disordered, and the foundations of human life would crumble. For example, if the governments of Europe had not withstood the notorious Attila, he would not have left a single living man.

Some people are like bloodthirsty wolves: if they see no punishment forthcoming, they will kill men merely for pleasure and diversion...

To recapitulate: the constitution of the communities depends upon justice, not upon forgiveness. Then what Christ meant by forgiveness and pardon is not that, when nations attack you, burn your homes, plunder your goods, assault your wives, children and relatives, and violate your honour, you should be submissive in the presence of these tyrannical foes and allow them to perform all their cruelties and oppressions. No, the words of Christ refer to the conduct of two individuals toward each other: if one person assaults another, the injured one should forgive him. But the communities must protect the rights of man. So if someone assaults, injures, oppresses and wounds me, I will offer no resistance, and I will forgive him. But if a person wishes to assault Siyyid Manshadi [A Baha'i sitting with us at table], certainly I will prevent him. Although for the malefactor non-interference is apparently a kindness, it would be an oppression to Manshadi. If at this moment a wild Arab were to enter this place with a drawn sword, wishing to assault, wound and kill you, most assuredly I would prevent him. If I abandoned you to the Arab, that would not be justice but injustice. But if he injure me personally, I would forgive him.

One thing remains to be said: it is that the communities are day and night occupied in making penal laws, and in preparing and organising instruments and means of punishment. They build prisons, make chains and fetters, arrange places of exile and banishment, and different kinds of hardships and tortures, and think by these means to discipline criminals, whereas, in reality, they are causing destruction of morals and perversion of characters. The community, on the contrary, ought day and night to strive and endeavour with the utmost zeal and effort to accomplish the education of men, to cause them day by day to progress and to increase in science and knowledge, to acquire virtues, to gain good morals and to avoid vices, so that crimes may not occur. At the present time the contrary prevails; the community is always thinking of enforcing the penal laws, and of preparing means of punishment, instruments of death and chastisement, places for imprisonment and banishment; and they expect crimes to be committed. This has a demoralising effect.

But if the community would endeavour to educate the masses, day by day knowledge and sciences would increase, the understanding would be broadened, the sensibilities developed, customs would become good, and morals normal; in one word, in all these classes of perfections there would be progress, and there would be fewer crimes.

It has been ascertained that among civilized peoples crime is less frequent than among uncivilized—that is to say, among those who have acquired the true civilization, which is divine civilization—the civilization of those who unite all the spiritual and material perfections. As ignorance is the cause of crimes, the more knowledge and science increases, the more crimes will diminish.

'Abdu'l-Bahá

References

1 *Promulgation of Universal Peace*, 'Abdu'l-Bahá
2 *Surah* II, 63
3 ibid., 8-18
4 *Newsweek*, Dec. 10, 2001, p.13
5 *Promulgation of Universal Peace*, 'Abdu'l-Bahá
6 *Citadel of Faith*, Shoghi Effendi
7 *Gleanings from the Writings of Bahá'u'lláh*, CXX
8 ibid, CX
9 ibid, CVI
10 *The Promised Day is Come*, pp.113-114
11 *Epistle to the Son of Wolf*, Bahá'u'lláh
12 *Gleanings*, Bahá'u'lláh
13 *History of the Decline and Fall of the Roman Empire*, vol. V, pp.462.
14 *Selection from the Writings of the Báb*
15 *Nabíl's Narrative*, p.605
16 *Gleanings*, Bahá'u'lláh, XXXVI
17 Shoghi Effendi, *The Advent of Divine Justice*, Bahá'í Publishing Trust, New Delhi, p.15
18 E.G. Browne, Introduction to "A Traveller's Narrative", pp.8-9, see *Nabíl's Narrative* p.663
19 *Promulgation of Universal Peace*, April 21, 1912, 'Abdu'l-Bahá
20 *Tablets of Bahá'u'lláh*, 71

21 *Secret of Divine Civilisation*, 'Abdu'l-Bahá
22 *Hadith*, the recorded sayings of Muhammad
23 *Bible*, Matthew, 22:37-40
24 see *Bible*, Luke 10:30
25 *Tablets of Bahá'u'lláh*, 28
26 *Paris Talks*, 'Abdu'l-Bahá
27 *Promulgation of Universal Peace*, 'Abdu'l-Bahá on May 24, 1912
28 Luke 11:41
29 John, 15:17-19
30 *Promulgation of Universal Peace*, 'Abdu'l-Bahá on May 24, 1912
31 ibid., May 2, 1912
32 *Paris Talks*, 'Abdu'l-Bahá, November 13, 1911
33 ibid., November 17, 1911
34 *Secret of Divine Civilisation*, 'Abdu'l-Bahá
35 *Proclamation of Bahá'u'lláh*
36 *Some Answered Questions*, 'Abdu'l-Bahá
37 ibid.
38 *New Testament*, John 7:16
39 ibid., John 8:40
40 *Promulgation of Universal Peace*, 'Abdu'l-Bahá
41 *Qur'án* 24:35.
42 *Secret of Divine Civilisation*, 'Abdu'l-Bahá
43 *The King James Bible* reads: "Ye have heard that it hath been said, Thou shalt love thy neighbour, and hate thine." Scholars object to this reading because it is contrary to the Law as set forth in *Leviticus* 19:18, *Exodus* 23:4-5, *Proverbs* 25:21, the *Talmud*, etc.
44 See *Galen Jews and Christians* by Richard Walzer, Oxford University 1949, p.15. The author states that Galen's summary here to is lost, being preserved only in Arabic quotations.

45 *Qur'án* 4:114
46 *Secret of Divine Civilisation*, 'Abdu'l-Bahá
47 Cf. Jurji Zaydan's *Umayyads and Abbasids*, trans. D. S. Margoliouth.
48 Cf. *Qur'án* 36:37.
49 ibid., 36:38.
50 *Galileo.*
51 *Some Answered Questions*, 'Abdu'l-Bahá
52 *Promulgation of Universal Peace*, Nov. 9, 1912, 'Abdu'l-Bahá
53 ibid., Oct. 12, 1912
54 Bible Isaiah, 23: 1:11
55 ibid., Acts, 3:016
56 ibid., Matthew 13:55-58
57 ibid., Mark 3:31-35
58 ibid., Matthew, 23:009
59 ibid., John, 20:017
60 ibid., Mark,11:026
61 ibid., Luke, 6:036
62 ibid., Matthew, 10:02
63 *Promulgation of Universal Peace*, 'Abdu'l-Bahá
64 *Bible*, John, 8:042
65 *Qur'án*, Surah 5:15
66 *MSNBC News Website*
67 *Bible*, Luke, 6:37-38
68 ibid., Luke, 18:10-14
69 *Qur'án*, LXII:1
70 ibid., XIX:111
71 ibid., XXXI:20,22
72 signed El-Hajj Malik El-Shabazz (Malcolm X)
73 *Bible*, Exodus, 31:15
74 Tabari, *Chroniques*, III, 202-203, cited in *Six Lessons on Islam*, by M. Gail.

75 *The New World Order*, p. 230, by Pat Robertson, Word Publishing Dallas
76 ibid. p.219
77 *Newsweek*, The Politics of Rage: Why Do They Hate Us?, Oct. 15, 2001 by Fareed Zakaria
78 *Newsweek*, How to Save the Arab World, Dec. 26, 2001, by Fareed Zakaria
79 *Qur'án* 39:12.
80 ibid., 41:53.
81 *Secret of Divine Civilisation*, 'Abdu'l-Bahá
82 *Qur'án* 59:9.
83 ibid., 26:84.
84 *Secret of Divine Civilisation*, 'Abdu'l-Bahá
85 see *Six Lessons on Islam*
86 *Qur'án* 42:43
87 ibid., 31:17-18
88 ibid., 16:126.
89 ibid., 24:35.
90 Dhu'l-Awtád is variously rendered by translators of the *Qur'án* as The Impaler, The Contriver of the Stakes, The Lord of a Strong Dominion, The One Surrounded by Ministers, etc. Awtád means pegs or tent stakes. See *Qur'án* 38:11 and 89:9.
91 *Qur'án* 20:46.
92 Cf. the Islamic confession of faith, sometimes called the two testimonies: "I testify that there is no God but God and is the Prophet of God."
93 *Secret of Divine Civilisation*, 'Abdu'l-Bahá
94 *Qur'án* 31:27
95 *Gleanings*, Bahá'u'lláh, p.136
96 *Qur'án* 5:14
97 ibid., 13:38
98 ibid., 6:103

99 ibid., 2:106
100 For Muslims interested in delving deeper into this subject matter pls. see, *Proofs from the Holy Qur'án regarding the Advent of Bahá'u'lláh*, by Dr. Sábir Áfáqí, published by Mir'át Press.
101 *Gleanings*, p. 217
102 *Epistle to the Son of Wolf*, pp.24-25
103 ibid. p.213